Who's Billy?

Denise Crooks

A catalogue record for this book is available from the National Library of Australia

Copyright © 2021 Denise Crooks
All rights reserved.
ISBN-13: 978-1-922343-82-6

Linellen Press
265 Boomerang Road
Oldbury, Western Australia
www.linellenpress.com.au

Dedication

This book is dedicated to the memory of my parents,
Ron and Gladys Crooks,
to Lorraine for giving me the drive and confidence
to write my memoir and
to my sister Annette, who rode part of the journey with me.

Contents

Contents	v
Foreword	1
Prologue	3
Chapter 1: Beginnings	6
Chapter 2: Settling	12
Chapter 3: Cray Fishing	33
Chapter 4: South Passage	44
Chapter 5: Work and Play	56
Chapter 6: Regular Army	62
Chapter 7: Army Reserves and 'Civvy' Street	86
Epilogue	107
Acknowledgements	108

Foreword

When I share stories about my early years in Australia, the first reaction of friends is to say, 'You should put those stories in a book.'

I toyed with the idea off and on over the years but didn't get serious until 2014, when I reconnected with a close friend, Lorraine. We talked for hours, reminiscing about the 'old times' and I told her stories of my childhood she hadn't heard before.

My inner voice became a persistent motivator, encouraging me to write my memoir.

There was one small problem that no one paid much attention to: I am not a writer. I came up with the idea for a working title easily, but didn't get much further until one day in 2019, when I met several friends for lunch, one of whom told us she wanted to learn how to write a book.

Here it is.

Enjoy.

Prologue

My highly tuned sense of responsibility and active curiosity haven't always been obvious, given my propensity to end up in trouble. Work colleagues, friends and family are often left bemused to ponder the dichotomy of my professionalism at work and the weird and wonderful predicaments I find myself in at home.

I'm never surprised at exclamations of, 'What have you done now?'

'Seemed like a good idea at the time,' is my stock reply, mostly accompanied by a wide grin, sometimes with a wide-eyed questioning look, posing an unspoken question in return, *Is there a problem?*

I have no choice but to acknowledge I have an uncanny knack of finding myself in the midst of mischief; I have to accept that is who I am, shaped by my upbringing, particularly during the first twelve years of my life when I navigated seismic shifts to my young universe.

The rounding of my shaping process continued with everyday life decisions I made and the consequences I had little choice but to manage.

I semi-retired in 2009 and moved to Geraldton. I kept three clients in my accounting portfolio, but, by 2012, the semi-retirement plan was shunted to the weekend. I changed my role from consultant accountant to full-time General Manager at a private medical business, during the construction of a new health centre – a far cry from my time as a driver in the regular army when I was nineteen years old.

In 2010, I joined the Women's Royal Australian Army Corps (WRAAC) closed Facebook page and reconnected with many of my old army pals, enjoying the chat and catching up with their news.

Home, in Geraldton, Western Australia, consisted of three ageing dogs – Bailey, Cosmo and Cheyenne. I found the demand for exercise and walk time wasn't high for the dogs or me. We were well set in our day-to-day routines, as well as night time organisation with Cheyenne at the foot of the bed, Bailey on the bed and Cosmo under the bed, contented by any measure.

I turned the computer off and joined the dogs in bed.

I couldn't sleep as my thoughts wandered to a good friend. I hadn't seen any posts from her on the WRAAC Facebook page. Nothing unusual as she might not be a member but I thought I would check next time I logged on … ask if anyone I was chatting with knew her, or if they knew what she is up to now.

The next day, I logged on and left a message. It was a couple of weeks before I got back to the Facebook page and I was momentarily surprised to see private messages for me before my memory jogged into gear. Two people replied they hadn't kept in touch. Thinking it was a dead-end, I put the idea on the back burner and forgot about it.

Two years later, I received a private message from a person who said she'd heard the friend I was asking about had married and now lived in Adelaide, South Australia.

The news kept percolating in my brain. Then a few weeks later I made my decision. Wouldn't it be great to catch up with an old friend, a good friend, and say hello? I sat down at the computer and searched the Adelaide White Pages. Typical. A lot of people in Adelaide had the same surname.

Take a punt. I picked six addresses and wrote a letter:

'Hello

I am looking for a friend who was in the army with me in the '60's and was wondering if she would happen to be a relative of yours ...'

I said I would appreciate any help they might be able to give and gave my email address, postal address and phone number.

Then I got on with my work and life.

***

I saw the envelope amongst the junk mail as soon as I opened the post box flap. At once, I was excited, curious and cautious, not wanting to get my hopes up but keen to open it. Cheyenne greeted me at the back door and had plans for playtime, so it was a few hours later when I finally discarded the latest weekly special fliers, put aside the local newspaper and picked up the envelope. I gazed at the postmark.

A letter ... a decision to make. A kaleidoscope of unrelated scenes swirled in my mind, back to a childhood adventure when I was four years old and met Neptune at the equator ...

Chapter 1: Beginnings

My birth, in July 1945 at Southend-On-Sea, was squeezed between two other significant events of that year, the end of World War II in Europe and the dropping of a nuclear bomb on Hiroshima. Amidst the horror and devastation in the world, I had little option but to bask in the loving care of my family and absorb their traits of resilience and hard work, as well as take in a good dose of humour.

As a nine-year-old, I was often in fits of laughter at the stories my mother told of her family during the war in London. I thought it wouldn't be so bad if another war broke out. From my naïve perspective, it seemed people found lots of ways to have fun. I remain ever thankful I have never had to experience, first-hand, the real bleak cruelty of war.

However, the first four years of my life in post-war Britain hold no clear memories for me; they are shaped by my mum's storytelling. Neptune's trident even gazumps the birth of my sister Annette in 1947. I was only two when she was born.

My mum's father, James Robinson, died when she was two-years-old and she grew up forging a close bond with her mother – nana to me – and three sisters: Elsie, Ivy and Vera. The war ravaged the family, with all three of my mum's brothers-in-law – airmen in the Royal Air Force – killed in action. My father, Ronald Crooks, a soldier in the British Army, was the only one to survive. Ironic in itself, he being the one family member at Dunkirk.

Post-war, my three aunts remarried. Elsie and Ernie continued to live in Southend-On-Sea while Ivy and Vera married Canadian-returned servicemen, subsequently moving with their husbands to Canada.

Mum told me I called my dad's mum 'Grandmother' as I thought her a stern, serious woman. When Mum gave birth to Annette at home, Grandmother took care of me and thought I would be better off with short hair, so she cut off my long ringlets. My mother was not impressed. However, she did have a kind heart and sent a telegram from me to my mother when Annette was born that read:

'I GOOD GIRL MUMMY. LOTS OF LOVE TO YOU AND MY LITTLE SISTER.'

My nana was very warm and soft, but she spoke funny. I found out years later that the treatment she received for throat and tongue cancer involved cutting out half her tongue. She died in 1949, and her wish to leave her body to science was fulfilled.

My dad, Ron, had the battle wits to present himself as a worthy suitor to Mrs Robinson's daughter Gladys. They were married in London on the 10th July 1940 when Ron returned from Dunkirk. They spent their first night in an air raid shelter. Two days later, Ron was deployed to Egypt. They didn't see each other again until November 1944. I arrived nine months later.

The first letter and decision to irrevocably change my and my family's lives was delivered in 1950 – we were notified of the approval from the Australian Migration Office to emigrate to Australia. My mum wouldn't leave England while Nana was alive but agreed with Dad, after her passing, to chase a better future in Australia than looked possible in post-war Britain. I was four years old, my sister, Annette, two years old, when our family left England from Southampton on the 30th March 1950, aboard the P&O Liner *Strathaird*, as full-paying passengers.

Mind you, I nearly didn't get on the ship. Elsie and Ernie took us to Southampton; Mum carried Annette onto the gangway, followed by Ernie carrying me. The ship's horn went off and I got the biggest fright of my short life, cried and put up a fight, not wanting to get on the ship because it made such a horrible noise. Needless to say, I lost the fight.

My mum was seasick throughout most of the journey, an affliction she passed onto my sister. I spent a lot of time at the swimming pool with Dad, who became an onboard hero after jumping into the pool and saving a child who had strayed into the deep end but couldn't swim. The ship docked at ports on the way, and Annette and I started to recognise the tell-tale signs that we would be going ashore. Mum would pack a few soaps and cloths. Annette and I would spend the day having our face and hands washed by Mum every time we touched anything. As we sailed across the equator, I met Neptune.

The ship was abuzz with excited kids, all dressed in an array of bright costumes, ready to meet the ancient God of the Sea. Annette wore the costume of a doll in a box. With the box fitted neatly about her waist, she paraded back and forth in front of her admiring parents and friends while I made sure I ate as much cake and ice-cream as I could.

Neptune came aboard with his trident. He met all the kids, giving each a personalized certificate, certifying their initiation as a daughter, or son, of Neptune and charging denizens of the deep to keep us safe should we fall overboard. We gave little thought to the logistics required to ensure we carried the certificate with us at all times, just in case we did fall overboard, nor whether the denizens would take the time to look for the certificate, nor, indeed, if they could read Neptune's charge therein …

As we sailed on the *Strathaird* across the Atlantic and Indian Oceans, the seeds of our family dynamics were sown. We were used to being part of a larger family. Now aunties, uncles, cousins were back in England, and we were a family of four. It was to be expected that Annette, as the youngest, would get more attention from Mum, but this was increased by the attention she needed to nurse her through sea-sickness. My mum stayed with her in the cabin when the sickness struck and nursed her through bouts of dry retching while struggling to keep Annette hydrated.

I was much more outgoing, partly because I didn't have a queasy stomach, but mainly because I loved being with my dad and playing with him in the swimming pool. Back in the cabin, Ron was concerned about Gladys and Annette. He would help by holding Annette while my mum had a break. I was shooshed away as they did their best to cope and look after Annette. I found ways to occupy myself.

The *Strathaird* docked at Fremantle on the 25th April, 1950. We were all very excited to get off the ship and looked forward to walking through town and soaking in the activity around us. Our excitement turned to bewilderment as we walked through deserted streets to our hotel. We knew little, if anything back then, about the importance of Anzac Day. We certainly had no idea that everything in Fremantle would be closed. Our hotel had no café or restaurant, no shops were open, and we had no supplies.

Annette and I sat quietly on the verandah of our hotel

room, confused and a little scared, as Mum sat and wept. Dad told us not to worry; he would go out and find us some food. He returned a long while later, and we tucked into our first meal in Australia – four packets of Juicy Fruit Chewies.

The next day was another first, when Mum went to the shop for milk, bread, butter and sandwich filling. She met the grocer who, she reported to my dad later, was a very kindly gentleman. They chatted about the family and our travels and he welcomed us to Australia. Mum asked for a pint of milk as they chatted.

'Where's your billy?' the grocer enquired.

Gladys smiled, thinking the man had got her mixed up with another family. She introduced us, 'We only have our two girls; this is Denise and here's Annette.'

'But you need your billy,' the grocer said.

Mum smiled and voiced her initial thought, 'You must have us mixed up with another family … just the two girls.'

'Well, there's a thing,' the grocer said. 'You can't get milk without your billy.'

'But who's Billy?' Mum asked. 'I don't know anyone called Billy?'

The grocer burst into laughter while Mum stood quite confused and getting flustered.

'But what do you mean, I don't know a Billy … why are you laughing?'

The grocer put his hand up. 'Wait a tick.'

He disappeared into the back of the shop and returned, holding up and waving a can.

'This is a billy. It's what I put the milk in. Everybody has one in Australia,' he said, grinning broadly.

Mum laughed, realising this was her first introduction to an iconic Australian word: billy, being short for billycan.

Mum bought a billy filled with milk, and we went back to the hotel to have a sandwich and tell Dad the tale.

Dad chatted to shopkeepers and others he met in Fremantle. He found out there were opportunities for work in Kalgoorlie, particularly in mining and prospecting. He and Mum decided to buy a car and caravan and go to Kalgoorlie.

Mum & Dad Wedding 10 July 1940

The house I was born in - 17 Victoria Drive, Leigh

Mum and I

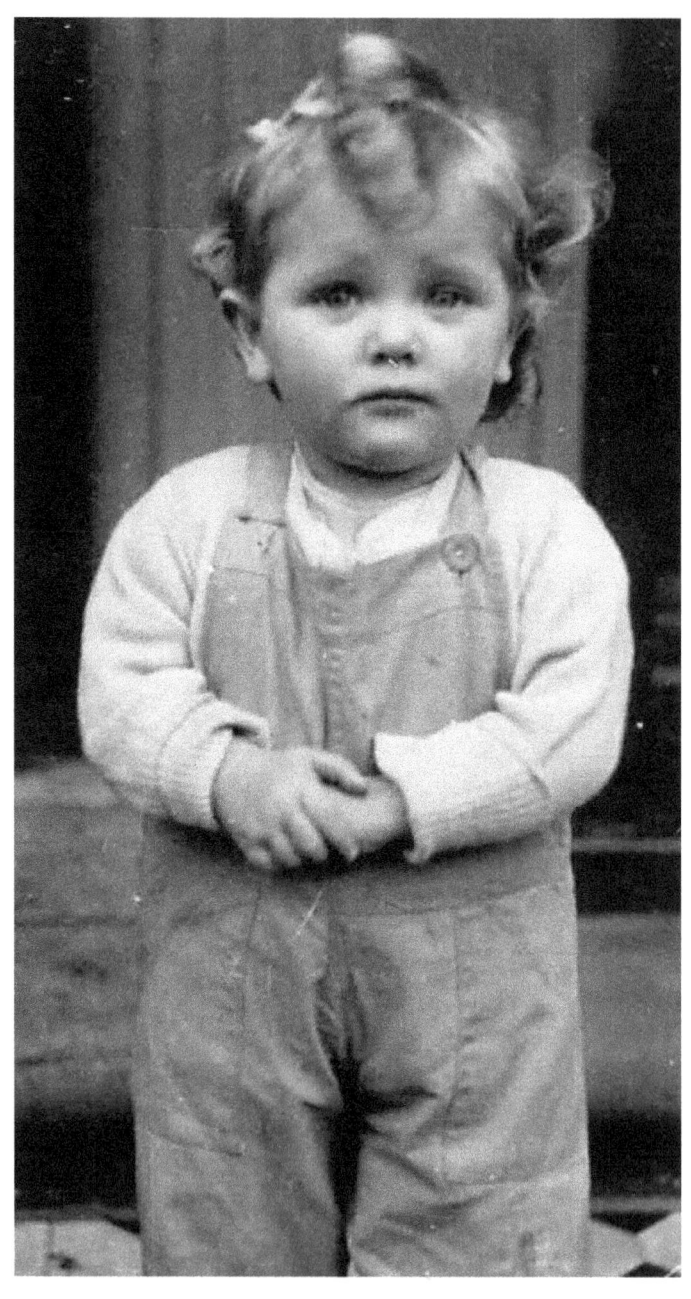

Me at 2 years old

Dad and I in England

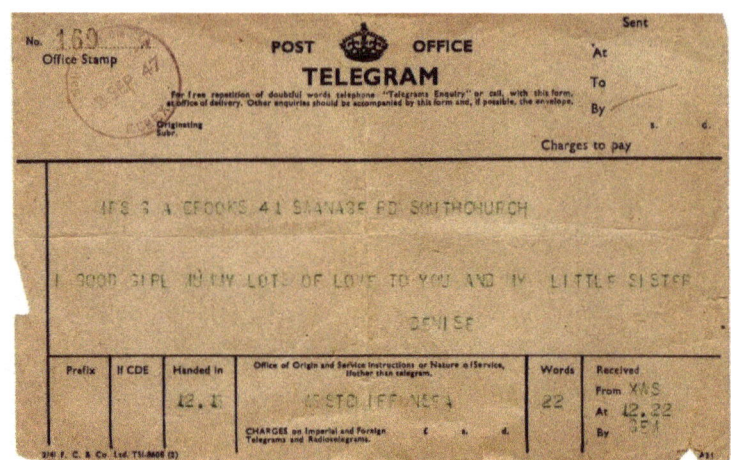

The Actual Telegram

On the ship

Annette and I on the ship

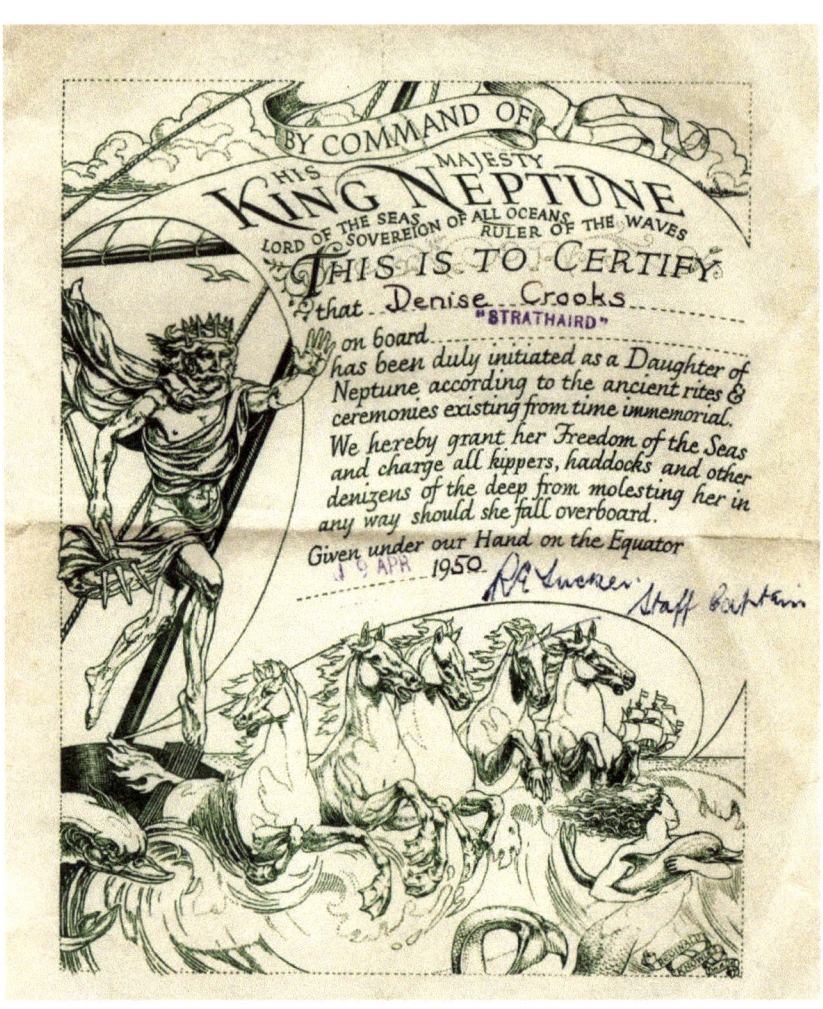

Chapter 2: Settling

Within two weeks of arriving in Fremantle, we took off, with the caravan in tow, heading to Kalgoorlie. Annette and I were typical siblings enjoying a long journey cooped up in the back of a car, alternately playing and fighting over important stuff like who could have the red lollies and who could draw the better horse. We were able to play and stretch our legs for half an hour while Dad changed a tyre, but stops were short. We kept moving, driving all day.

We stopped for fuel, and Dad asked the man whether we were nearly at Kalgoorlie.

'No, mate, you're thirty minutes out from Geraldton. Kalgoorlie is about 550 miles that way,' he said, pointing south-east to a destination at least a ten-hour drive in the opposite direction.

Somewhere on the road to Kalgoorlie, we had taken the wrong turn and ended up going north.

It was nine o'clock and dark by the time we parked, on the beach, at the Geraldton Caravan Park. We were all in bed and asleep in no time.

We woke to Mum saying to Dad, 'Isn't it nice to wake up to the sound of the ocean?'

Annette and I jumped out of bed to be with her as she opened the caravan door.

She started yelling, 'Ron! We're in the ocean. Save the girls. I can't swim.'

Dad had managed to park on the beach a tad close to the water's edge and the tide had come in, taking us a little way into the Indian Ocean. There were a lot of people on the beach laughing.

The odd comment reached our ears. 'Bet they're stupid poms.'

Nevertheless, a few of the men organised vehicles and pulled the car and caravan out of the water, back onto dry beach.

We never did get to Kalgoorlie.

Dad decided to look for work as our money was dwindling. His first job, working for the railway out in the middle of nowhere, took him away from us for weeks at a time. We dressed in our best clothes on a Sunday to visit him and the other dads, with families from the caravan park who shared the same predicament.

Mum cried at the conditions he was living in. The camp was a patch of dry, dusty dirt, housing six small canvas tents shared by the workers as sleeping quarters. Drinking water, stored in a 44-gallon drum, stood in the sun; food, a generous description, consisted of salted meat and canned food, both broiled on an open fire. Dad washed in a basin of cold water, and the surrounding bush served as his toilet. Workers were never alone, hundreds of flies their constant companions everywhere they went.

Mum was relieved, as was my dad, when he got a job carting wheat closer to Geraldton.

Mum and Dad made a huge effort to save what little money they could afford. Dad was soon able to set himself up in his own business as a qualified spray painter and panel beater, a qualification he achieved in England after the war. He hired space at the Geraldton Building Company, a one-stop building and manufacturing centre directly employing around 600 people and housed, as well as contracted, many self-employed tradesmen. He quickly established a solid reputation, and at last enjoyed his work.

Back then, you had to turn six years old before you went to school, which meant I couldn't start school until July 1951. So, my first months in Australia were spent playing on the beach and eating lots of watermelon.

We used to play on the dinghies anchored in the shallows of the bay, Annette happy they were nestled in the sand. One day a young boy pushed one of the dinghies away from the shore, unaware Annette and I were lying in it. Annette, feeling the increased rocking of the dinghy, sat up and shoved me to get up. We jumped out of the dinghy, not realising the boat was now in very deep water. Annette couldn't swim. She kept flailing about, gradually sinking. Her head went underwater. I managed to grab the side of the dinghy to keep myself afloat, then grab Annette by the hair and pull her head above the water. I had no choice but to hang onto her hair and the dinghy. I yelled and screamed for help. A man heard us and came to our rescue.

Next day, the story made the front page of the local paper. Mum and Dad were very proud of me, but we were still told off and warned about playing on the dinghies. Annette reaffirmed her dislike of the water.

Dad loved fishing. I followed him around when he came home, eager to go with him. On our first fishing expedition together, we caught quite a few little fish, and I knew what we could do with them.

'Mum, Mum. Look at the fish we caught. We can have them for dinner,' I said excitedly.

'Oh, look at you. Look at all the fish you caught,' she said.

'Hmm, I think they're a bit small. We have to clean them first and there won't be much left to cook.' She saw my disappointment. 'I know … why don't I cook them for Tibby?'

Tibby was our adopted cat.

'Yes,' I shouted. 'I'll help.'

We cooked up the fish and I watched Tibby devour her tasty meal. Afterwards, she licked her lips and slunk off to her bed, a cat box Dad made for her.

The next morning Mum called Tibby. When she didn't appear, my mum went looking for her. She found Tibby in her bed, curled up, quite dead.

Chatting to one of our neighbours, Gladys described the fish cooked up for Tibby. She found out about pufferfish, locally known as blowfish. One pufferfish contains tetrodotoxin, a deadly toxin, enough to kill thirty adult humans. There is no known antidote. Gladys was relieved we hadn't eaten them. We would have gone the way of the cat.

The day arrived for me to go to school. Mum had been talking up about how good it would be at school for me now I was a big girl. She made me a new dress and bought me a new school case. She chatted on about looking forward to watching me walk into school and having the opportunity to meet other mums.

The big day arrived and heralded an eventful first week at school. Unfortunately, Annette was sick and Dad was at work. Mum was faced with little option but to put me on the bus and stay home to look after Annette. Mum packed my pens and pencils, along with a lamb sandwich, cut into four squares wrapped in greaseproof paper, into my school case. At the bus, she asked Margaret, a friend we played with at the caravan park who had started school six months earlier, to look after me as it was my first day at school. Mum waved me off, and I watched as she turned to hurry back to the caravan, tears running down her face.

The school bus was very old and rickety, with beach sand all over the floor dragged in from our shoes. I sat down on a seat, put my school case on the floor and spent the short trip looking out the bus window. Unbeknown to me, one of the kids unclipped my school case, so when we arrived at Geraldton Primary School, I picked up the case only to have everything, including my sandwich, which had now come out of the greaseproof paper, fall into the sand on the bus. Much to the amusement of all, including Margaret, I did my best to gather everything as kids laughed and pushed past me to get off the bus and run through the school gate.

By the time I had picked everything up, everyone had disappeared into school. I walked through the gate and stood in the empty playground, looking up at the large formidable building. I was scared, with no idea what to do or where to go. I kept standing there. A teacher came out and asked what I was doing. She led me to my classroom, only after I overcame my shyness to tell her it was my first day and I didn't know where to go.

I was told I had to take threepence with me the next day to pay for The School Fund. Mum duly gave me the money. The teacher started going around the class collecting everyone's threepence. I was so nervous, I kept twisting the coin in my fingers, and for some inexplicable reason I put it in my mouth. The teacher came closer. Her hand, palm up, came towards me and I swallowed the coin. The teacher was more concerned about me choking than about the coin itself. She called me a silly girl and told me to bring another threepence with me the next day. To this day, I have no idea why I swallowed that coin.

Once home, I told my mum what happened and she laughed. 'We'll just have to wait 'till it comes out, won't we?' she said.

The afternoon wore on and I started to complain about an ache in my tummy. When my temperature went up and the pain worsened, Mum called the doctor. The doctor said my appendix was about to burst and I was rushed off to the hospital. The surgeon got rid of the offending appendix and returned the threepence he found lodged in it. At least we got the money back.

I was a newly arrived 'Pom', naïve to Australian ways, small for my age and very shy and quiet, traits that didn't last long. A few of the older kids were quick to start calling me 'the pommy'. The way they said it, I knew they weren't being friendly. One of my new friends told me it was because I spoke with an accent. From then on, I hated my accent because it made me different, so I set about losing it. I listened to the other kids speaking, and when I was by myself, I mimicked the sound of their accent, repeating phrases over and over. It wasn't long before I spoke with an Aussie twang.

The other thing I practised, testing my mum's patience, was the national anthem, God Save the King. When King George VI died in 1952, the words of the national anthem became God Save the Queen. I was very confused and got the words mixed up on a regular basis. For a seven-year-old replacing all the hims with her and kings with queen was quite a challenge.

One or two kids added trailer trash to their heckling and

my friend told me it was because I lived at the caravan park. I had no idea what was wrong with living in the park. I always wore clean clothes, I was polite, always had a packed lunch. Their words hurt, but there was nothing I could do, so in the end, I ignored their taunts.

Many years later I learnt 'Pom' is thought to be a short form of pomegranate, reflecting its skin colour in a nickname for British immigrants, referring to their sunburnt and ruddy complexions. At the time, being called trash was certainly worse than being likened to a fruit.

The first week at school was hard, but it served to nurture the seed of self-reliance in me. I learnt, during that first week at school, to not overly trust nor put too much faith in people. The other trait nurtured in me as a positive consequence is when people do stand-up and prove themselves to be trustworthy, I am a loyal and dependable friend.

We lived at the caravan park for twelve months, the time it took to save enough money to buy a block of land on Johnson Street, in the suburbs of Geraldton. Dad built a room onto the side of the caravan that served as our kitchen and living room. He installed a wood stove but had to pull it apart and start again as Mum couldn't get the door open.

Annette and I explored the block and set about getting used to playing on grass. Annette was out playing one day with the boy across the road, whose family owned the local dairy. They were playing with matches and managed to set the block on fire. It was quite a big thing as the fire engine arrived, which drew many spectators.

Away from the caravan park Mum and Dad met new people and were soon invited to casual drinks, birthday parties and barbeques. The first invite arrived with a request to bring a plate.

Mum was concerned the family had to ask you to bring your own plate. In an effort to help out on the day, she took all our plates and knives and forks, no food. There was much hilarity when another Aussie term was explained. 'Bring a plate' means to take food to share to contribute to the feast. Mum didn't make that mistake again.

The area around Johnson Street wasn't heavily built up, and there was a paddock at the back of our block that housed a very large, black bull. One day, Annette and I decided to go and meet the bull. We set about talking to it, and it started snorting. We thought this was hilarious and started skipping back and forth singing to it. Needless to say, we had no idea it was getting mad until it took off and ran at us.

We screamed and ran toward the caravan where mum had a sponge in the oven. We ran inside and slammed the door shut, just as the bull went thundering past, onward and out into Johnson Street. What with slamming the door and the bull thundering past, the sponge in the oven went flat. Mum, again, wasn't happy. Neither was the owner of the bull, nor the police and helpers, whose unenviable job it was to catch the rampant, angry bovine. The bull was moved to another paddock, and Dad fixed the fence. We laid low for a few days.

Dad was doing well with his spray painting and panel beating business and more saving, along with money from the sale of the caravan and our block, got us into a position to afford to buy a four-room house. It was only a short distance from Johnson Street at 240 5th Street in Wonthella, the inner northern suburb of Geraldton not formally gazetted as such until 1972.

Mum needed a washing line, so Dad made one for her. He

even made the prop, a long piece of wood with a 'V' shaped end, to hook onto the line to push against the weight of the wet washing, lifting it higher into the wind.

Annette and I made tracks with our bicycles as we raced around the block. One day we went off track and knocked the prop over. Mum was not happy when she discovered the freshly washed sheets trailing in the dirt.

I was surprised when, many years later, I visited my aunts in Southend-On-Sea in England, to find they still used props on their washing lines. In Australia, we had become accustomed to the Hills Hoist.

Annette was now six-years-old, and ready for school. We were both enrolled at the Allendale Primary School located in the same street as our new home. Annette settled into school life quickly, which meant Mum didn't have to take her every day. Annette and I started walking to school together. The school wasn't completely finished and, because I was in a different year than Annette, I was bussed each day with our teachers to different schools in the area.

A polio epidemic swept through Australia in 1956 and a countrywide vaccination program was introduced late in the same year. Every Tuesday for six weeks, the entire school student cohort was marched from Wonthella to Geraldton Hospital to be vaccinated. Not long after our treatment ended, the one dose drop of the vaccine on a lump of sugar was introduced.

At our school, one teacher taught two grades, both groups in the same classroom. I was always more interested in the grade higher than my own grade, and positioned myself in the middle of the room so I could follow the higher grade work put on the blackboard. I was fortunate one of my teachers,

Mrs Carter, saw I liked and was good at mathematics and coped with the higher-grade work. I was allowed to skip a couple of grades and Mrs Carter took a special interest in teaching me extra math.

I became a successful accountant, travelling the world with my various jobs. I often reflect on the time and care Mrs Carter gave me and regret I didn't have the opportunity to thank her personally. I would have liked her to know how well I had done in my career and how she helped me get there.

Our daily family routine consisted of Dad going to work, Mum packing me and Annette off to school and family time in the evenings. While our days and months were happy and carefree, they were overshadowed by Mum's unhappiness. She missed her family terribly, and letters between the siblings didn't fill the void for her. It was nineteen years before Gladys was reunited with her sisters. Ivy and Vera joined her and Elsie in Southend-On-Sea for the reunion.

During school holidays, all our friends, parents and kids, would visit their relations 'down south' for holidays. We didn't have any relations in Australia, so we stayed home. Mum's routine didn't change much at all, except she was lonelier. Annette and I tried to amuse ourselves. I came up with the bright idea to ask Mr Smith if I could go with him on his rounds. He delivered bread with his blue cart and white horse. I don't know who was more surprised when he said yes – me, him or the horse.

Annette would never stray far from Mum so she stayed home when I went off every day of the school holidays. My job was to move the horse forward while Mr Smith delivered the bread, then giddy-up the horse when he got back on the cart. Mr Smith lived in 6th Street, and every lunchtime we would stop at his house under a tree. He fetched water for the horse then went inside to have lunch with his wife. He never once brought or offered me a drink. I often wonder if that was a ploy to have me wander back home, but it didn't work. I was bored at home and liked being with the horse, we were great friends.

Our house was very small, with a lounge room, kitchen, two bedrooms, one bath and toilet. Our water was heated by a chip heater, a popular way to get hot water in Australia from the 1800s until the 1960s. It used to take ages for the water to heat up and fill a bath deep enough to get in and get washed. By the time we coaxed the fire with newspaper, bits of wood and anything else we could find, there would be more ash in the bath than hot water.

Dad decided it was time to make our house bigger and have a separate shower and bath with a modern electric water heating system. He enlisted the help of his friend, Max Cramer, and soon work was in full swing. When they finished, we had a large kitchen, three bedrooms and the now enclosed back verandah became the laundry and the bathroom, with a separate shower and bath - all with hot and cold running water.

Mum loved her new house and was very proud and happy. While she missed her sisters in England and Canada, she settled into the Australian way of life. Until Dad came home one day very excited about a new venture.

I doubt he was aware of the full extent of what was to come.

Leaving Perth with our car and caravan

Watermelon on the beach

Caravan with Room Johnson Street

Wonthellla house when bought

Wonthella House renovated

Mum and the Car

Chapter 3: Cray Fishing

Dad, to us, seemed happy in his work but his adventurous spirit took over the day he had a serious chat with Mr Mullins, a local cray-fisherman. The chat turned into a business deal, where Dad swapped his successful panel beating business for a cray boat, a shack and jetty at Big Rat Island in the Houtman Abrolhos Islands. The Abrolhos is a chain of 122 islands and coral reefs in the Indian Ocean, declared a national park in 2019. Ron had always liked the sea, and it made sense to him that here was an opportunity. There were no second thoughts about swapping his business for a cray fishing boat, shack and jetty – despite his knowledge of the industry being less than zero …

He chatted to other cray fishermen to pick up tips of the trade.

He told Gladys, 'They go out early each morning to pull their pots, re-bait them and put the pots back in. Then they return to port 'till the next morning.'

'Only once, every day?' she queried.

'Yes. Lazy if you ask me. They could go out again in the afternoon and pull the pots. They'd get more crays.'

A few days later, someone kindly explained to him the crayfish only crawl at night. Lesson learnt.

The day before he took over the cray fishing business, I went with him to his work shed. He was making new cray pots. Seated atop a pile of wood, I was working my way through a bag of jubes, Dad's favourite lollies, when Dad, cutting batons on a band saw, got distracted and took his eye off what he was doing. The band saw kept working and went through his thumb. The thumb had a tenuous link to his hand, just hanging on. I got such a fright I popped all the jubes, except one, in my mouth and offered the last one to Dad.

'Not just at the moment, love,' he said.

He grabbed a piece of cloth, wrapped it around his hand and we took off to the car. The cloth was soon soaked with blood and he tried to stem the bleeding by putting pressure on the makeshift bandage by holding it tight with his other hand.

'C'mon, Denise, on my lap,' he said, sliding into the driver's seat. 'You steer.'

He started the engine, slammed it into second gear, put pressure on the accelerator and we were off. I sat on his knee and hung on to the steering wheel for grim death, my whole body moving with each turn, while Dad shouted instructions, *left, right, straight along…* I steered the car alternately onto the footpath, then out wide on turns, all the way to the doctor's surgery. Dad stopped the car as I mounted the pavement for the last time.

I pushed the car door open, jumped out and raced into the surgery, screaming, 'My dad is dying.'

Dad didn't die. His thumb was saved. It was a few more years before I again drove a car in the streets of Geraldton.

Our fishing boat was called *Chiquetta*, and Dad decided to take the boat and his family to the islands as soon as possible. He sailed *Chiquetta* to Rat Island then met us at Geraldton to collect us and our belongings on the *Lady Joyce*. We arrived at Rat Island on the return journey of the *Lady Joyce*, a carrier boat used for transporting fish caught by commercial fishing boats.

We encountered rough seas on the crossing. Mum and Annette reacquainted themselves with their nemesis, seasickness, while Dad and I ate vegemite sandwiches. We took our two cats, Ginger and Boko, along with our galah, Pinky. Pinky was in his cage, stored in the hold. The cats, in their crates, were on the deck with us, almost going overboard on more than one occasion. Annette and I worried about Pinky during the rough crossing. We went to check on him, opened the hatch and there he was, out of his cage, sitting on some bags singing, 'Dance cocky ...'

Mum, still feeling the effects of the rough crossing, was shocked when she saw, and then stepped into, the shack. Our new home was a weatherboard building divided into three tiny rooms. There were two bunks at one end of the bedroom, a double bed at the other. A wood stove stood in the centre of the kitchen, with room enough for one person to stand at any given time. We had no running water or electricity. The toilet was a hole blasted into a large coral outcrop overhanging the ocean, with a wooden structure built around it. We called it the outhouse. The description of 'toilet' was in deference to the toilet seat perched on top of a small wooden box placed strategically above the hole inside the outhouse. Our very own thunderbox!

Mum had little choice but to adapt to the living conditions and, for a short while, cope with her and Annette's seasickness as the three of us became Dad's deckhands. Ron knew nothing about the waters around the Abrolhos and we kept running up onto sand bars. Mum, Annette and I helped by getting into the water to push and rock the boat free, while

Dad handled the engine and barked orders of when to push and when to rock. Of course, the other fishermen referred to us as the 'stupid poms', but that all changed when Ron got the hang of it and became a very good cray fisherman.

He soon learned how to manage the boat himself, and we were left to spend our days doing our schooling via correspondence and playing on the rocky coral shore we loosely called 'the beach'. I enjoyed the school work and would get it done quickly, but Annette was easily distracted, so Mum had to spend a lot of time pushing her through it.

Besides watching us with our school work and doing the daily cooking, which was hard work as she had to cart and boil the water when needed, Mum spent time sewing and keeping the place clean and tidy. She made a set of curtains to hang on the front of tea chests, laid on their sides which were used as cupboards.

On the side of our shack was a lean-to where Annette and I used to play shops with our tinned food supply. One day we got sick of selling the same tinned food, so we took the labels off the tins to make up new tasty delights to sell. That evening Dad, Annette and I, sat at our small kitchen table while mum cooked dinner, getting very frustrated because she was struggling to find a tin of peas. With the labels gone, she had to guess which tin held the peas based on the size and colour of the tins. It proved a fruitless exercise because she kept getting anything but peas.

Dad said, 'God, woman, you don't know if you're Arthur or Martha.'

Annette joined in and said to Dad, 'Well, you don't know if you're half a watermelon.'

We froze and looked at Annette. Dad looked puzzled.

Mum raised a questioning eyebrow.

Annette said, 'Well, you just told mum she didn't know if she was half a tomarta.'

Once Dad taught me how to skull a dinghy, which became my preferred mode of transport for my exploring. Annette didn't venture far from the shack and wouldn't go anywhere near the dinghy because of her sea-sickness, which meant I had to keep myself occupied. I didn't mind, having learnt not to rely on others from my experiences in the caravan park and the first week at school. I loved the quiet and peacefulness being in the dinghy fishing, or simply basking in the sun, floating on the water. Just me and the ocean. I was happy and becoming my own person. The fishermen would wave as they sailed by and I never felt alone.

Laurie, our next-door neighbour, used our jetty. I used to wait on the jetty for him to come in, and would jump onto his boat and help clean it. One day he was tinkering with the engine.

'Denise, hold this lead for me while I turn the engine over.'

'Sure,' I said and took the lead.

He turned the engine key. I got a shock and almost went over the side of the boat. I was holding the spark plug lead and was given a solid kick. Laurie almost fell overboard, laughing. I am a fast learner, and I made sure I never fell for that trick again.

One day, I encouraged Annette to come with me to our pontoon, a very large floating box where the crays are kept until they can be taken to Geraldton. At the pontoon, I gave her the mooring rope and told her to jump off the dinghy onto the pontoon and tie the rope. As soon as she was on the pontoon, I pushed the dinghy away. I had untied the rope on the dinghy. I left her there and went back to the jetty. I am sure folk in Geraldton wondered where the screaming was coming from. Mum ran to the jetty and was horrified to see Annette siting on the pontoon, screaming and crying.

Mum told me in no uncertain terms to go and get her. 'Immediately!'

'But she is annoying me, so I don't want to get her,' I said.

Mum won the day and I got her back. However, that did it for Annette. She refused to go in the boat with me again. It was probably also the defining point for our relationship growing up. We love each other as siblings do, and support each other always, but we manage to irritate each other on a regular basis. We are opposites in many ways, with a magnetism that pushes towards argument as opposed to mutual respect.

I knew, from an early age, Annette was Dad's favourite, and she would use his affection to great effect. She would start arguments, or pester and annoy me to the point we would descend into fighting. Dad would tell us to stop it. Annette would cry and say I started the fight, and Dad would smack me. Mum was the peacemaker, loving us both equally. I was always a bit of a loner. The more I spent by myself, the more my self-reliance grew, as did my curiosity and mischievous behaviour.

One day, while exploring in the dinghy around the island, I had a lucky escape. I momentarily lost my bearings and decided to float for a few minutes under the shade of an overhanging rock. Something plopped in the water next to the boat. I knew at once where I was, sitting directly underneath a thunderbox. Another plop and a shower of pee just missed me as I skedaddled out of there.

Mum found the correspondence schooling more challenging than she expected, particularly when Annette got into the habit of tearing up the papers. The decision was made and, in April 1954, we were returned to Geraldton and went back to school.

Arrangements were made for us to live with a family in the next street, 6th Street, directly behind our house. We were warmly welcomed by Aunty Joy, Uncle Phil and their three boys. Mum returned to Rat Island with Dad. We didn't have a choice in the matter. I found the separation difficult at first but gradually settled into the adventure. Annette hated the experience and missed her mum and her dad terribly.

Aunty Joy was a strict disciplinarian, which was just as well, looking after five kids, each one year apart in age. The eldest was Trevor, aged ten. I was next soon-to-be nine, then Brian aged eight, then Annette six and a half, and Graham aged six.

The house was a lot smaller than ours at 5th Street. It had one bedroom, a tiny lounge and a moderate-sized kitchen at the back. We kids slept on the front verandah, which had a canvas awning we could pull down to protect us from the weather. I loved it out there – it was like camping. The house had no running water, and the kitchen housed a wood stove, table and chairs. There was no sink or refrigerator. The combined bathroom, laundry and toilet, were on the back verandah, only partly partitioned.

We all had our chores to do. The chooks had to be fed and eggs collected; wood chopped; the very large vegetable garden weeded and watered. Dishes were washed in a basin atop the kitchen table. Hot water from the kettle was poured into the basin over a bar of soap housed in a tin with holes in its base.

With chores done and dishes washed and put away, it was

our turn to bathe. Aunty Joy's chores and everything else, was done with military precision, including the evening bath. We each got one dipper full of hot water from the copper, lit earlier in the day, and tipped it into the bath. Then we got in and washed, youngest to eldest. Graham's bathwater was notoriously shallow but clean. Trevor and I had a deeper bath but added our share of grime to already dark water. We were then marched into the kitchen and sat on the kitchen table while Aunty Joy examined us to make sure we didn't have any scrapes or 'Doublegee' points in our feet. Doublegee is a significant weed in Western Australia, it forms seeds with three sharp woody spines that easily dig into bare feet. They can leave tiny points in your flesh if they snap off rather than being pulled out, resulting in painful sores.

We ended the day listening to "The Burtons of Banner Street" on the radio with Uncle Phil, and when that was finished, Aunty Joy tucked us into bed.

Once a week, Uncle Phil killed a chook. Our job was to pluck it before it was cooked in the wood stove. It was yummy. We spent our week when not at school making kites and flying them in the paddock. I would play with them for hours. If anyone did anything wrong and we tried to blame each other, we all got told off and sent to our beds to read.

There was a slight change to our routine as winter approached. We each wore a camphor block tied with string around our neck after we'd dressed for school and had eaten breakfast. After breakfast, we had to line up in front of the fire, eldest to youngest, and each given a teaspoon of treacle and garlic. The camphor block was removed before we went to school. Both of these treatments were designed to stop us getting influenza. Nowadays, it is recognised that camphor can be toxic to young infants and children if absorbed in large enough quantities through the mucus lining of the nose and mouth. Nevertheless, the smell of the garlic and camphor combined was enough to ward off a marauding army, never mind enterprising bacteria and viruses, and we came to no harm.

The four months we lived with Aunty Joy and Uncle Phil was tough because we missed our parents, but we were well looked after, never hungry and I loved Aunty Joy.

By the end of July, Mum and Dad returned and took us home.

Dad arranged to moor and continue cray-fishing from Geraldton in the off-season until the island season in March. When Dad went to the islands this time, Mum stayed at home and Dad visited every month for a couple of days. I felt sorry for my mum and would sit with her on the front step, my nine-year-old arm around her waist. I knew she really missed Dad.

In the evenings, she, Annette and I would sit around the woodstove and play games and cards. Annette, always the clown, often emptied the cupboards of various items and put them in a suitcase and come into the kitchen as a salesman and try to sell her wares. We laughed a lot, particularly when Mum told stories about the war years in Southend-On-Sea.

Both my mum and Annette were afraid of the dark, so I became their protector. If anyone knocked at the door, I was the one to answer it. Mum and Annette peeked out from behind the kitchen door.

After school, I used to chop the wood then go to the shop to get anything we needed. One day, my mum sent Annette to the shop for a packet of raspberry waffles. She came back with rice and apples. The shopping stayed my responsibility.

The Shack at Rat Island

Me as Miss Muffet in school play

Me at School

Chapter 4: South Passage

In 1955, Dad sold the boat, shack and jetty at Rat Island and bought a bigger boat, *Falcon*, as he wanted to try the cray fishing in South Passage, the channel between the southern point of Dirk Hartog Island and the Western Australian mainland. Dad wanted Mum to go with him, which meant Annette and I went as well.

Mum didn't want to leave us with Aunty Joy again as she'd had a bout of tuberculosis and only recently came home after being away for six months for the treatment. The plan was to stay at Shelter Bay, 138 miles from Denham, accessible by sea. There was no access via road or track, and it felt like the middle of nowhere, which it probably was back then. I don't think anyone had ever lived there before we arrived. Maurie Glazier, a friend, joined us on the adventure with his cray fishing boat.

Our gear was packed onto *Falcon* in Geraldton, and Dad sailed to Denham. We drove – a long trip on gravel roads, but we made it in one piece. We stayed one night at the local hotel owned by Mr & Mrs Glass before we boarded *Falcon* the next morning and headed for South Passage. We made good time and moored at Shelter Bay with plenty of daylight for Dad and Maurie to unload all the gear, including our new home, a large canvas tent.

The tent was large enough to house a double mattress on a frame held off the ground by four 12-gallon drums, two camp stretchers, one either side of the mattress, for Annette and me and one small table with four chairs.

A smaller canvas tent became the kitchen and housed all our food supplies and cooking equipment. Our water supply sat in a 44-gallon drum, with a pump attached. Dad and Maurie buried a large ice chest in the sand to store perishables, but it didn't work very well, so our meat was salted. Our bathroom was an aluminium basin, our toilet the bush. Mum worked hard at keeping our space as tidy and clean as possible, even going so far as brushing the sand around the tent to keep it neat.

Dad's big blue wooden toolbox was the first item off the boat, and Annette and I were told to sit on the toolbox, not to move and stay out of the way of the activity. Annette had other ideas and wandered off. I was unusually obedient and sat and waited. I heard a noise, a distinct rustle behind me.

My head was already turning to the sound as Dad shouted, 'Don't move!'

Too late. From the corner of my eye, I saw a huge snake, and I was off and running as fast as I could down the beach before the words were out of my dad's mouth – what a welcome from the locals.

Mum did all the cooking on a single burner kerosene primus stove. The lighting process involved pumping the stove while you lit the wick. Mum kept fumbling her way through the process, and it wasn't unusual for the stove to tip and start to burn the tent. Most times, Dad was there to quickly put the fire out.

One day Annette and I were lying on the beach when we heard Mum yelling. Dad was out fishing. It looked like the whole tent was on fire. I grabbed an empty sack, ran to the water, soaked it then ran and threw it on the burning tent. We did put the fire out, but one side of the tent was gone. By the time we left Shelter Bay, only five months later, there was barely any tent left.

I spent most of my time at Shelter Bay exploring the beach and the offshore reef not far from our campsite. My kit was a beanie, water bottle and a fishing knife in a pouch hooked on my belt. There were many giant turtle shells along the beach that I would roll over and play with. On the reef, I would prise oysters off the coral with my knife and sit there and eat them. To this day, I love fresh fish, and I make a very tasty sea-food pizza. Mind you, one meal fostered in me a dislike of one specific part of a fish.

Shelter Bay was a popular mooring place for the large boats used by line-fishermen, either as a stop immediately before a long fishing trip or as a rest stop on their way back to port.

One day, Dad came home and told my mum we had been invited by a Captain Dad had met several times to join him and his crew onboard one of the boats for a meal. Mum declined the invitation. The thought of attempting to eat a meal on a rocking boat was enough to make her feel queasy for the rest of the afternoon.

I excitedly agreed to go with Dad when he asked me if I would like to go with him. We took the dinghy and clambered onto the boat. The captain met us and took us down into the boat's galley. It was hot, stuffy and smelled of fish and diesel. The feel of the boat rocking on its anchor was more pronounced below deck, and I thought Mum had made a good decision to stay on solid ground.

I listened to the men chat while they prepared the meal.

The first course arrived. I looked at the plate, then gave a wide-eyed look at Dad.

He smiled at me with eyebrows raised and his lips pursed in a 'Yum, that looks good,' pose.

When I didn't look away from him, he nodded to my plate and delivered the unspoken message, 'Just eat it.'

I looked back at my plate and stared at three toothpicks stuck into three fish eyes; I swear they were staring back at me.

I gingerly picked up a toothpick; the fish eye didn't drop off. I raised the fish eye to my lips, then quickly sucked it off the toothpick and swallowed. I did this three times. I can't say I tasted anything, but I can say I have never eaten fish eyes since.

The galley became hotter as the cooking progressed. The fish and diesel aroma, now enhanced by garlic, and the boat kept rocking so I was relieved when I saw and tasted the next course, very tender and tasty crumbed meat and garlic. I was surprised when a third course arrived, and it wasn't a dessert. A big bowl of spaghetti and meat sauce was put in front of me, which I duly ate.

I was pleased there was no dessert, because I wouldn't have been able to squeeze another morsel past my lips.

The time arrived for us to leave. We stood. I waited. The boat kept rocking while Dad shook hands with each of the men.

Once on deck, I managed to say, 'Dad, I'm going to be sick.'

I raced to the side of the boat, just in time to lean over the rail and purge the entire meal from my stomach into the ocean. The food was in such a hurry to escape that bits of spaghetti found their way out via my nasal canal – an experience not quickly forgotten – and for a long while I blamed the fish eyes, sure all would have been well if I had left them on the plate.

My most important job at Shelter Bay was to take Dad in the dinghy to *Falcon* and pick him up to bring him back to shore when he returned from fishing, five hours later. One day I went exploring and found a cave that I just had to check out. It was so cool I decided to stay in there for a while. I paddled in the shallows of the cave and fossicked through the shells at the water's edge. I figured it was about time to go home to pick up Dad, so hopped back into the boat and went to go home. I couldn't get the dinghy out of the cave as the tide had risen. I had the sense to tie the dinghy to a rock at the back of the cave, then swim home.

Mum saw me walking back to the tent. 'Denise, you're wet. Where's the dinghy?' she asked.

'It's in the cave back there. The tide came in and I couldn't get it out,' I explained.

'Oh,' she said. She looked to where Dad was mooring *Falcon*. 'I'll be in the tent.'

I stood on the beach, nervous and a little scared of what would happen next. Dad beckoned me to come and get him. I shook my head, held my arms out wide and shrugged my shoulders in a 'can't do' sort of gesture. He was getting annoyed, his waving more insistent. I kept shaking my head. He had no choice but to swim. As he drew closer, I backed away. He was wet, tired and not a happy man when he finally got to shore.

I told him where the dinghy was. He ranted and raved for a few moments, then looked at me.

'It's alright, love. You'll go get it in the morning,' he said.

I was sent to rescue the dinghy at 03:00 the next morning,

in time to take Dad to the moored *Falcon* when he was ready to start his day. I made sure it didn't happen again.

Dad would often let me go with him, and I found out how impatient cray fishermen are. He did everything at speed, as though something was about to descend on the boat and sweep him away before he got the pots rebaited and back in the water. The first time I decided to help, I heaved and pulled on a pot rope. I was exhausted by the time Dad saw me and came to my rescue to get the full pot back into the boat. I did get the hang of it, although I spent most of my time on the boat fishing. Which came with its own challenges.

It wasn't unusual for the pots to be full of octopus, colloquially known as occys. Dad used them for bait. He would grab an occy, cut its head off and throw it behind him onto the deck. He would forget I was there and it wasn't unusual for me to be splattered with dying octopus.

I would let out a loud 'Aw yuk, Dad,' while frantically brushing their squirming tentacles off me.

He would turn, look at me and say, 'You'll be alright, love.'

We went into Denham every two to three weeks to pick up supplies and check the mail. Mum always made sure we were spick and span in our good clothes, the only ones washed in fresh water. Our everyday clothes were washed in salt water. One day we were dressed and ready to go to Denham. Mum wore a lovely summer dress she kept for special occasions. The four of us got settled in the dinghy to take us to *Falcon* but our collective weight meant it got stuck in the sand. Dad asked Mum to hop out and give it a push. The dinghy broke free so fast that she fell face-first into the water, her nice clean summer dress now drenched and sandy. Mum popped her head up out of the water with a look of thunder. Dad, Annette and I were scared to speak. We endured a very quiet trip to Denham that day.

To many, our time on Rat Island and Shelter Bay sounds carefree and idyllic, but I doubt Mum would agree. Both places had their challenges in basic living, complicated by having two children to supervise, including the school work by correspondence. Many times, Annette got hers and tore up the papers. I was off exploring and Mum had no idea where I was. While at Shelter Bay, I took myself over to Dirk Hartog Island on several occasions and didn't tell my mum or dad. Thankfully I managed to get myself out of the odd scrape and was very fortunate to avoid getting into trouble on the crossing to the island – the waters of South Passage are renowned for being dangerous. If there had been an accident with the dinghy, or Dad's or Maurie's boat, with neither in close range, we would probably still be there.

We had been at Shelter Bay for five months when we went on a supply run and received the second letter that changed our lives. It was from the Education Department: Annette and I had to go back to school. I think Mum was relieved as she decided to stay home with us while Dad kept fishing South Passage for a few more months.

The waters around South Passage can be treacherous and showed Dad just how bad it can be. He was pulling pots one day when the *Falcon* was hit by a breaker. Maurie was close by and rescued Dad from the water. *Falcon* joined a myriad of whalers, cargo boats, fishing boats and pearl luggers at the bottom of the ocean.

Dad bought another boat, *The Islander*, and moved from South Passage to once again moor and fish from Geraldton.

I used to help Mum as much as I could when we were on

the Abrolhos Islands and at Shelter Bay, and I continued this when we went back to Geraldton. I resented being told not to do something when my dad was home; he would look after this or that, and it wasn't unusual for Dad to be quick with his hands to slap me away. I was too young to fully appreciate that I felt left out, and I wasn't the head of the house when Dad was home. Truth be known, I wasn't the head of the house with Mum, but I felt a lot more useful and important when my dad wasn't there. Mum did rely on me for a lot of things as I was one of those kids who was 'ten years old, going on sixteen'.

Dad didn't settle for long and decided to try fishing in the Gulf of Carpentaria.

When Dad was in the Gulf, money became very tight, so tight we often didn't have any, and there were many things we could no longer afford, including food. My mother was amazing; she could make many tasty dishes with potatoes, and in my own way, I tried to help.

An old man lived at the corner of our street. He was once a keen gardener but, as he became older and his health declined, the garden was left to do its own thing. There were lots of vegetables in the back yard being eaten by the birds, so I knocked on his door.

'Hello, I live a few doors up and saw you had lots of vegetables in your backyard. Can I go and pick some?' I asked.

'No, you little upstart, bugger off,' he replied and slammed the door.

Not to be deterred, I waited until the next day and watched till he wasn't home. I jumped over the fence into his yard and picked what I wanted.

'Here, Mum,' I said, handing her the vegetables. 'The man

at the corner house gave them to me.'

She didn't find out I pinched them and the old man didn't miss his vegetables.

The butcher was diagonally across from our house and he would give free bones to people with dogs. I popped into the shop one day and asked, 'Can I have some bones for our dog, please?'

'You don't have a dog,' he said.

'We do so too,' I replied indignantly.

He wasn't sure, but he gave me some bones. I failed to elaborate our dog had died some twelve months earlier.

Mum unwrapped the package, and yes! there were dog bones, lots of them, great for soups and stews, along with three pieces of steak. Mum made me take the steak back to the butcher, thinking it a mistake.

I reluctantly returned the meat.

'No mistake,' he said. 'I put the steak in there for you and your family.'

He did this on several occasions, a wonderful man.

Mum got a casual job at Coles. She worked Thursday, Friday and Saturday mornings. Annette and I helped by cooking dinner for mum every Friday night, so she didn't have to cook when she got home from work. Mum gave us big hugs and told us every time we cooked how much she enjoyed our meal. We cooked the best chips, eggs and peas. **Every Friday**. Years later, she fessed up and said she was sick and tired of eggs, chips and peas. It was a meal we regularly ate, not just on Fridays.

One school holiday period, I helped out with money by getting a job in a crayfish factory bagging and packing cooked crayfish. I worked 5pm to 7am for two shillings an hour. It was really hard work but I dug in, happy that I was helping Mum.

When Dad came home from the Gulf, he bought a new boat, *Compass Rose*, and continued to crayfish from Geraldton. Once my dad was home, Mum and he would often throw parties and invite their friends, and they would all sing and dance on the verandah. I would get out of bed and open my door a crack and watch all the dancing.

On one occasion, Dad had too much to drink. I lay in bed listening to the sounds of my mum cleaning up, my smile fading as I heard Dad shouting. Mum came into my bedroom and locked the door. She climbed into bed with me. Dad shouted at the door, then started to kick it. I thought the door wasn't going to last the onslaught, so I ushered Mum out the window. I followed, and we ran to the front of the house where I climbed through Annette's bedroom window, then ushered Annette out the window to Mum. It was pitch black. There was no moon, and the street lights had gone off at midnight. We walked into town in our pajamas and sat on a park bench until daybreak. Mum told us to stay put and went back home to find Dad asleep and everything, including the bedroom doors, in one piece. She returned, with Aunty Joy, in her car and took Annette and I home. I am relieved to say such an episode was never repeated.

Once back at school, Annette developed a new role for me. She managed, on several occasions, to get into some argument or other with the kids in her class. I shouldn't have been surprised, given how often we slipped into fighting about something at home. However, instead of standing up for herself and dealing with the issue she helped create, she would say, 'My sister will bash you up at the break.'

The first time it happened, I stepped out of my class and walked into three or four kids wanting to fight. That was the first and only fight. Other times, I talked myself out of the situation, which was just as well, as Annette didn't stop holding me up as her fight master, despite many arguments at home and warnings from Mum and me to stop.

Annette and I would get pocket money for doing chores, not that Annette did many chores. Annette would spend her pocket money in the first couple of days, whereas I would put most of mine in my money box. Annette knew I always kept my money in my money box. One day she pestered and pestered me to give her some money, and I wouldn't. Dad got tired of listening to her whining; he got my money box and broke it open and gave her the money. He told me off for not being willing to share.

Despite some tough times, I had an amazing childhood full of adventure and laughter with the best parents you could wish for. They would always make Christmas the most wonderful time. Annette and I felt special, waking on Christmas morning with a pillowcase each at the end of our bed, overflowing with gifts. We would grab our pillowcase of goodies and run and jump into bed with our mum and dad and open our presents. We had the biggest smiles and felt so very loved.

One Christmas, I got a brand new bike that had gears. I took it for a ride and, when I got back, Annette said,

"Let me have a ride."

I said no but she pestered until Dad told me to let her have a ride. Reluctantly, I handed the bike over and told her not to touch the gears. About fifteen minutes later, Annette came back pushing the bike, with the chain in her hand.

During the first five years of Dad's cray fishing business, we went through significant changes. From the isolation of the Islands and Shelter Bay to the separation from both Mum and Dad, followed by Dad's variable absences. All of the experiences, good and not so good, taught me to stand on my own two feet and helped me develop inner strength and resilience. I learnt how to be resourceful and to not be afraid to ask questions, however cheeky they might be.

At the end of the high school year, there was a Founder's Ball for all the students. Mum bought me a new dress and shoes and I learnt to dance. I was so looking forward to my first ball. The night before the ball, I asked Annette to practice the dance with me. We were in the kitchen, where Annette managed to get me backed into the cupboards. She kicked my foot, breaking a couple of my toes. The night of the ball, I sat on a chair at the edge of the dance floor, looking a picture wearing my new dress, one new shoe and a clean, fresh bandage on my broken foot.

I finished my first year at high school, topping all the exam scores. At thirteen years of age, I knew Geraldton wasn't for me. I wanted adventure in my life, and I wanted to travel but needed a bit more study and work experience to help me on my way.

Chapter 5: Work and Play

I chose to enrol in the business course at Stella Maris College staffed, managed and run, by catholic nuns. My tutor was Sister Ursula, who, I thought, was cranky. She wasn't cranky mad, just very strict. As an example, another girl and I were not catholic, so Sister Ursula had us stand outside every morning while everyone else went to catechisms. I never understood this – surely, God wouldn't have objected to us joining in.

There was no such thing as a computer back then, just very large ledger books for your figures. You had to transcribe the numbers neatly, with pen and ink, a blotter close by to reduce work being smudged. I admit I was a neat freak with my ledgers.

Sister Ursula had the unfortunate habit of spitting when she spoke. One day, as she walked around the class checking our work, she came up behind me. I immediately closed my ledger to prevent any wayward spittle finding its way onto the pages. I waited for her to walk on and sat twirling my ruler. She leant over my shoulder, grabbed the ruler and snapped it. I snatched the two pieces back and broke it into another couple of pieces.

Without hesitation, she said, 'Go outside, Crooks, and stay there until you have more sense.'

I stayed outside for a short while, waiting to be allowed back in. Nothing happened, so I got on my bike and went home. The next morning, she stood me at the front of the class. I could see she was angry.

'Yesterday I sent you outside. You were nowhere to be seen when I went to get you. What do you have to say for yourself?' she demanded.

My classmates stared at me.

I girded my loins and said, 'You sent me outside until I had more sense. After a short while, I didn't have any more sense so I went home.'

The class burst out laughing. I was sent outside again.

I was fourteen years old when I left Stella Maris College at the end of 1959, and started working in Coles after my mum put in a good word for me with the manager. The Coles stores had separate sections and counters with different products. I started working in the Hardware section before being transferred to Toiletries and Cigarettes. Within two weeks, I was promoted to head of that little section. At fourteen years of age, I was the youngest to hold the position of Head girl at Coles.

I stayed at Coles for eighteen months before moving to St John of God Hospital as a nurse's aide in the maternity section, with a grand wage of £5.6 shillings per week. I really loved and enjoyed the work and used to get really excited when I was in the delivery room, watching the birth of a child. It was so special, and the nuns were so much more fun than I had experienced at Stella Maris College.

I was enticed by a wage increase to move to the Geraldton Regional Hospital and worked again as a nurse's aide until June 1964. I then earnt £17 per fortnight.

Mum had taught me how to drive years before, in our big black Oldsmobile. We used to drive up and down our driveway. Reverse and first gear were all I knew until she took me to a road out of town. She sat me on cushions until I had a reasonable view through the windscreen, then I was put through the paces of learning the finer art of gear changing. Getting my feet onto the pedals was a challenge. The method that worked best was to slither my bum side to side across the cushions and stretch out either my right or left foot till they touched the pedal and the operation completed.

Left bum cheek across and forward, left foot stretch, push the clutch. Shift the gear stick a notch. Slither my right bum cheek across and forward, right foot stretch, press the accelerator. My waist muscles got heaps of exercise. I loved the experience and pestered my mum to take me driving at every opportunity.

By the time I was fourteen, boys had become interesting beyond being school mates. Mum and Dad thought it would be easier to keep an eye on me by making sure I invited my friends to our house.

I enjoyed dancing and used to go to the Learners' Session at Druids Hall every Monday night for ballroom dancing lessons. My passion, however, was Rock & Roll. I had learnt how to jive, and I practised with the fridge door as it was solid and didn't fall. Mum wasn't too impressed, worried the door would drop off with all the opening and closing and the fridge losing its cool. I thought the only one really losing its cool was her. We created parties with a handful of people. We had room to dance, and my mum would put on plenty of food. Mum and Dad joined in with the dancing, they were both very good dancers and could jitterbug all night, and all the boys joined in because Mum and Dad made it so much fun.

They were great hosts – all my friends loved their company. At the weekends, a group of us used to go to the local dance at the yacht club, then go to Jack Snacks for toasted chicken sandwiches, often ending up at my place afterwards. We had lots of parties and everyone was invited.

One Christmas, Annette met the members of a four-piece band and invited them home to be our entertainment for the party. Mum invited a couple that she worked with, Rae and Bill, for a quiet drink on Boxing Day. By the time they arrived, the party was in full swing. Mum opened the door to welcome them in.

'Come for a quiet drink, you said. I couldn't even get parked in the bloody street,' Bill said with a huge grin on his face.

My boyfriend at the time was Kevin, who owned a Zephyr. He used to let me drive, and I drove all over town and never got stopped or caught for not having a driver's license. Mind you, we were always with two other friends and Sprog, who owned an FJ Holden ute. We preferred Sprog's FJ Holden because it had a radio. The five of us would squeeze into the front bench seat with the radio turned up. Having a radio in your car was a big thing back in those days. Most cars, including Kevin's, didn't have a radio.

The day after my 17th birthday, my mum took me to the Geraldton Police Station.

'Morning, Constable Rudd,' I said.

'What can I be doing for you two ladies today?' he asked.

'I'm here to take the test for a driver's license.' I said.

He raised his eyebrows. 'But I've seen you driving around town for a couple of years now.'

I nodded and fessed up that I wasn't old enough for a license until yesterday, my seventeenth birthday.

I looked younger than seventeen, and my parents were surprised and relieved that I hadn't been stopped or questioned about driving. Nevertheless, I passed the test and got my license.

Of course, now I had my driver's license, I wanted my own car. Mum and Dad said they would go to Perth and get me a second-hand car, so I gave them the money I had saved: £480 sterling. They went to Perth while Annette and I stayed home, taking the opportunity to continue our partying while they were away.

Mum and Dad returned with a second-hand Consul. I asked if my £480 was enough as I was hoping for some change. They said yes, it cost exactly £480, which was a fair price in those days. The car was on the train due to arrive in a couple of days. I was so happy when it arrived, my first car, it was heaven. Many years later, I wondered if it was really £480 or was it more and they had never said anything?

One night I drove Mum, Annette and I to the movies. Once the movie was finished, we hopped into the car to go home. I pulled away from the curb and proceeded to do a U-turn. I didn't see the oncoming car, but felt it when the cars collided. Neither of us was driving fast so we avoided a big accident and no one was hurt. However, the front of my car had been pushed onto the wheel. A group of boys standing nearby saw the mishap, and one of them came over and freed the front wheel for us. His name was Frank, nineteen years old, and a cray fisherman with his own boat. I started dating Frank, and we were inseparable.

I was seventeen, driving legally, and hadn't stopped looking for opportunities outside of Geraldton.

Annette was now working as an apprentice hairdresser and came home with a different colour in her hair every week. One weekend she was practising cutting hair on Mum and accidently nicked the bottom of mum's ear. Mum's ear started to bleed profusely.

'Oh! Don't worry, Mum,' said Annette. 'I'll just cut straight across your ear. It's already cut halfway.'

Me at 16

Chapter 6: Regular Army

Family military connections were strong in my family, given the not so distant memories of World War II. I wanted to experience life outside Geraldton and travel, and looking back, it seemed an inevitable step to join the army and follow in Dad's footsteps.

I didn't talk about my decision with Mum and Dad until I had all the paperwork to join when I was seventeen. If you were younger than twenty-one years of age, your father had to give his approval by signing the documents.

'Dad, I got my papers today to join the army. Will you sign here for me so I can get them sent off?' I said, pointing to where his signature was needed, thinking there would be no problem.

'No, love. I think you should wait. Bring them back to me next year,' he said.

I was disappointed but didn't argue and, with little option, I determined to wait.

On my eighteenth birthday, I pulled out the papers. 'Here, Dad, you told me to wait. Please sign them.'

He looked at me and slowly shook his head. 'No, love. You can do much better with a job. Look at the opportunities you have with your certificates.'

'But, Dad, I really want to join, please sign.'

He refused, and suggested I wait another year and, in the meantime, look for a better job.

I didn't want to wait so I enlisted my mum's help. It took six months, but, in the end, Dad was convinced. I had my fingers crossed my application would be in time for the June 1964 intake.

I sold my Consul and bought a new Ford Prefect – a black Ford Prefect, with a silver swan on the bonnet, whitewall tyres, and a radio. I used to wash and polish my car almost every time I drove it. I loved my car, and everyone knew it was mine.

I was still working at the Geraldton Hospital and would occasionally give friends or neighbours a lift to the hospital before my shift. One day, I had an older lady in the car. I was on a slip road heading onto the main drag into town. There was a give way sign so I slowed and checked no cars were coming and continued onto the main drag. After a few minutes, and a long way further down the road, I saw the flashing blue lights of a police car and was waved down.

A young policeman approached the car, and I wound down my car window.

'You failed to give way,' he said.

'No,' I replied. 'I slowed to check for any vehicles then continued safely.'

'You could have caused an accident. You didn't give way,' he said.

My passenger spoke up, 'You're mistaken officer … she slowed down, and she did check to make sure the road was clear.'

'Besides,' I said, 'there aren't any cars on the road. How could I almost cause an accident?'

"I'm charging you. You should have taken more care.' He wrote out the ticket, went back to his car and drove away.

I chose to ignore the matter, so got a shock when I was informed by a patient it was in the newspaper. I lost my license for three months for reckless driving.

I received the third letter to change my life in April 1964 to advise that my application had been reviewed and accepted. I was required to be in Perth on 4th June 1964 to enlist. I joined the Australian Army eight weeks short of my nineteenth birthday.

My boyfriend, Frank, helped me pack and spent a lot of time with me. We talked about our future, and I agreed to marry Frank at the completion of my three years enlistment. Mum, Dad, Annette and Frank took me to the bus station and a few friends were there to wave me on my way. I left Geraldton giving strict instructions Annette was not allowed, under any circumstance, to drive my car.

Once in Perth, I went to the Army Recruitment centre in William Street and underwent the mandatory medical and physiological tests, which I passed with flying colours. I was one of six recruits from Western Australia who took the Oath of Allegiance and became members of the Australian Army on June 4th 1964. We were subsequently transported on the midnight flight from Perth to Sydney to join other recruits flown in from around Australia. In Sydney, the female recruits were loaded into an army bus and taken to Georges Heights to undertake the six-week Army Recruit Training Course, or boot camp as it is fondly referred to. I soon found out why.

The weather was wet and windy on our arrival in Sydney, worsening as we drew closer to our destination. The rain poured down, supported by a chilling wind, as we disgorged from the bus.

We were greeted by a big female sergeant major barking

orders: 'Come on, hurry up, line up here. Single file. Get a move on. You,' she pointed at me, 'help her,' pointing at another recruit. 'Start passing ports from the bus.'

I had no idea what she was talking about. A port, to me, was something by the sea where you tied a boat. The water pooling at our feet didn't exactly meet the criteria of a sea.

I turned in time to catch the first suitcase she, the other recruit, threw at me. I passed it to the person next to me. The process continued while the sergeant kept barking orders. The rain drenched us as the cases, ports, were laid out across the wet road.

'Pick up your ports,' the Sergeant Major barked. 'Move to the barracks on the right.' She pointed the way. 'Move it!' she yelled. We didn't need a lot of encouragement, eager to get out of the rain.

My clothes were soaked through. I was cold. I now knew a port is a suitcase, and all I could think was, 'What on earth have I got myself into?'

Women's Royal Australian Army Corps – WRAAC School as it was known – was a very large military base at Georges Heights, the location used by the military since 1871. WRAAC was formed in 1951, with WRAAC School, after a short time at Mildura, conducted in two locations, Georges Heights Sydney, and Crows' Nest Military Camp, Queenscliffe, until 1984. Post-1984 training of female recruits was integrated as a whole of Army training at other centres based on their trade specialty.

The barracks at Georges Heights consisted of five rows of five rooms, with three beds in each room. There was a long verandah along the outside of each row, with an ablution block in the centre. The location of Georges Heights on the ridge of Sydney Harbour, near Mossman along the Lower North Shore, effectively captured the oncoming sea breezes, contributing to the belief the parade ground was the coldest, windiest place on earth.

On our first day, we were each allocated to a room, shared with two people, and we chose our area with a bed, a desk and small wardrobe. Our temporary kit was issued: shoes, stockings, cardigan and what was called a GD (general duties) dress.

For six weeks, our days were filled with learning to march, learning to salute and classroom time learning about the Army and what was expected of us. To ensure we mastered the technique of saluting whilst marching, we had to salute the flag pole every time we passed it. To ensure we mastered marching, we marched. We were not allowed to walk anywhere, only march.

During the first several days at WRAAC School, I was finding my bearings. This was the first time I had been away from home, living by myself – well, at least outside of the family daily routines and structures. I could hardly call sharing a building with thirty other women as living by myself. Nevertheless, as I was finding my feet. I conducted myself with a quiet demeanour. I was eager to learn and, despite the repetition, I enjoyed class time and marching.

One day on the parade ground, the Corporal controlling our platoon's marching session was momentarily distracted as she answered an officer's query about our progress. Without another order, the platoon kept marching, straight ahead, off the parade ground, down the hill and into low bushes that scraped and tore at our legs. We kept going. Directly in front of me was a small tin shed, no wider than three feet.

Too late, the Corporal realised the front of the platoon had disappeared from sight.

'Halt!' she yelled.

The few lines at the back stopped, but the recruits at the front, including me, didn't hear her.

She yelled a second time and most of the remaining platoon members heard and stopped. But I didn't hear the order, so didn't.

I marched straight into the shed and at the back of the shed I kept marching, marking time.

The Corporal ran down the hill and started shouting.

'Private Crooks only, halt.' I heard her, then followed the rest of her commands. 'About turn, ten paces forward, halt. About turn. I was back in line. We were still facing downhill.

The order came, 'Platoon. About turn.'

We faced in the right direction. I was now in the back line of the platoon.

'Platoon, quick march,' came the order, and up the hill we went.

I constantly had a sore arm with every injection known to man given to the new recruits. I am not sure what I expected when it came to food, but I was pleasantly surprised when I entered the mess hall for my first meal in the Army. Roast beef with five vegetables. I enjoyed the meals during recruit training, all the meals except breakfast, that is. Breakfast was predominantly bacon and eggs – powdered eggs with bacon cooked in a tray by pouring boiling water over it.

During the first week, we were taken by bus into the city to be fitted for uniforms. They were all tailor-made back then and given to us during our last week of training. I felt so proud and wanted to wear my uniform everywhere.

The completion of recruit training was marked by a march out parade past the Commanding Officer. Dressed and marching in our new uniforms, we completed our drills with precision, and I enjoyed celebrating our collective achievement at graduation.

After the march out parade, we were notified of our new postings. I was posted to Mount Martha in Victoria. The news was bittersweet, exciting to be going somewhere I hadn't visited before, but sad as many of the women I had befriended were off to different postings.

I arrived at Mount Martha in mid-July 1964; my role was GD (General Duties). The work was straightforward as there were five GD's: mop the passageways, work in the kitchen, clean the ablutions and the sergeants' mess and help in the kitchen as required. I had the work done most days by 11am.

By the time I arrived at Mount Martha, I was confident, committed to the Army and comfortable in myself. I was always very professional in my approach to work but the old adage of work hard, play hard suited my personality. I soon made friends, and we found many ways to get up to mischief.

Julie's room became the place to congregate, being the room best situated amongst our group, on the outside wall of the building. Julie also had a Berko camp cooker so we'd gather to play music and cook fish fingers and other tasty delights.

You needed a pass to be able to leave the barracks, particularly at night – a rule we didn't always follow. Many a night, we snuck out the window from Julie's room, just to get out and go for a walk. Mount Martha wasn't renowned for its buzzing nightlife; there was only one little shop. One night on our return, I was sent first to climb back through the window to Julie's room. All went smoothly until I realised it wasn't Julie's room. I had successfully climbed into the bedroom of our RSM (Regimental Sergeant Major). Julie and the others realised the mistake and left me there; ran to the correct window; climbed in and were out of sight by the time the RSM looked outside to see if I had any companions. I was confined to barracks for the next week.

We did do the right thing at the weekends and got passes to go to Frankston. We would visit the bowling alley or have lunch at the pub. The only minor problem: we managed to avoid getting into trouble about drinking before the legal age of twenty-one.

On occasion, I was called upon to work in the kitchen to assist when an Officers' Dinner was held. On one such occasion, I was carrying a large pineapple stuffed with cream and other fruits and was weaving my way through the dining room when a male Sergeant came up to me and squeezed my backside. Without hesitation, I landed the pineapple in his face. I was charged.

At the resultant hearing, I explained the circumstances. The charge was dismissed, and the prisoner – me – returned to normal duties.

In December 1964, I was notified that I had a new positing to Northern Command Trade Training Centre (NCTTC) in Brisbane as the unit driver.

I was able to fly home for leave at Christmas and looked forward to seeing my family and friends. Frank picked me up at Perth airport and we drove back to Geraldton. After sharing all my news with Mum and Dad, I ran outside and hopped into my car. I immediately knew something was amiss. Something didn't smell right. The smell was fresh paint.

I went back inside and asked Mum what had happened to my car. She explained Annette was trying to help and was only backing the car out of the driveway. She had not driven in a straight line and managed to catch the side panel along the hook of the gate clasp, ripping a large hole along the side of the car. Dad had fixed the resultant hole and the dents either side of the hole.

I went out again visiting friends. Then I returned home, I found Annette going through my case. She spotted the red blouse I'd bought just before leaving Mount Martha.

'Oh, can I wear this?' she asked.

'No, I haven't worn it yet. I'm saving it for the New Year's Eve party,' I said, taking it from her and hanging it in the wardrobe.

Later that evening I got dressed and Frank and I went out. When I got home, I saw Annette was wearing my new red blouse. In the ensuing fight, my new blouse was torn. I never got to wear it.

It was on this, my first trip home, Frank and I had a long talk. We decided absence doesn't always make the heart grow fonder and decided to end our relationship. It was obvious that a small town and marriage was not what I wanted.

Immediately following the New Year celebrations, I was flown from Geraldton to Perth, then Perth to Brisbane. The flight was long, uncomfortable and hot.

I was rationed and quartered at 10 WRAAC Barracks, 17 Laurel Avenue, Chelmer and bussed to Northern Command Train Training Centre (NCTTC) in Enoggera daily.

I was in awe at the very large and imposing building that housed 10 WRAAC Barracks and decided to look into its history. The land and building, leased to the Australian

Military Forces in 1950, was occupied by the 10 WRAAC from 1 April 1953. The original owner, thought to be Thomas Beevor Steele, built a substantial, middle-class residence on the property stretching from (what is now) Laurel Avenue to the Brisbane River. Title to the property passed in September 1913 to Alison Eavis Harding Frew, a prominent Queensland civil engineer, who resided there until circa 1940.

In December 1940, the use of the house and land, of almost 1.4 hectare, was transferred to the Australian Red Cross Society with title formally transferred in 1947. The Society converted the house into the Lady Wilson Red Cross Convalescent Home, providing for the rehabilitation of Australian soldiers, sailors and airmen, returning from the battlefields of the Second World War. The name of the home was in honour of Lady Wilson, President of the Queensland Division of the Australian Red Cross at the time, and wife of His Excellency Sir Leslie Orme Wilson, Governor of Queensland.

Conversion of the house into a convalescent home required alterations and additions to internal partitions in the main residence, and construction of a substantial dormitory block behind and parallel to the main house, which is where my donga (living quarters) was. In the early 1950s, the convalescent hospital was closed and the property leased to the Australian Military Forces.

I was met at the steps of this historic building by the then Commanding Officer, Warrant Officer Townsend, who took an immediate dislike to me. She eyed me up and down, gave me a curt nod.

'Follow me, Crooks,' she said with obvious distaste in her tone.

She led me through the main building and over a walkway to a dormitory, out onto an open verandah and showed me a bed. This was my new sleeping quarters, a bed with a mosquito net hung from the roof of the verandah. There was no protection from the weather, no cooling system, not even a fan.

The building backed onto the river. At dusk, the area was inundated with mosquitos. It wasn't unusual to find evidence of possums on the bed, cute to see them scampering through the palms, not so cute catching them scurrying away from your bed.

Soldiers and staff were still on leave, so there wasn't much activity around the barracks. The unit I had been posted to wasn't due to open for another week. With nothing to do, except lay on my bed, I occupied myself by reading. I suspected Townsend didn't appreciate the inconvenience of having to accommodate a Private that wasn't part of her own unit, nor to find space in her full barracks.

There were two dormitories, each housed ten personnel. An ablution block stood between the dormitories. As everyone returned from leave, the dormitories quickly filled and were full of noise and laughter. I soon started making friends. I found out that all of us quartered here, with the exception of the 10 WRAAC Barracks driver, were bussed every day to our respective units. My theory in regards to Townsend didn't wash. I wasn't particularly upset about her attitude towards me, but I did find myself treating her routine orders with a tad degree of belligerence.

I had recently completed an army driver training course to take up my posting as a driver for NCTTC. I drove a Land Rover. I really didn't have to do a lot except drive the

Commanding Officer, a Captain Simpson, around as required, pick up supplies and run errands. I met Lorraine Fuller, who was the WRAAC Barracks driver, and we became fast friends, spending a lot of time together. We were such close friends, Lorraine came with me to Geraldton to celebrate my 21st birthday in 1966. It was during this trip my curiosity was piqued by my mother.

My mum was interested when she learnt Lorraine's surname was Fuller, because her mother's maiden name had been Fuller. We didn't go into any other discussion on the topic while in Geraldton. On our way back to Brisbane, we stopped in Adelaide for Lorraine to spend time with her family and celebrate her 21st, which was 10 days before mine.

Once back at the barracks, I did some digging and found out that Lorraine's grandfather was my mum's uncle. I didn't know he'd also emigrated to Australia and settled in Adelaide, South Australia. Lorraine and I were second cousins. Lorraine didn't know that side of her family.

One day a telegram arrived for Lorraine. The officer of the day opened it. Before delivering it to Lorraine, the officer contacted my officer in charge, who ordered me to return to barracks. They knew we were good friends and that Lorraine needed support.

The telegram delivered the sad news that Lorraine's grandmother had passed. I sat with Lorraine. She was very upset, as she was close to her grandma. In the end, the only thing I could think of doing to cheer her up was to take her to a party. Later Lorraine told me it worked a treat.

By the time I returned to barracks at Chelmer each evening, I was invariably light-hearted and cheerful; no tiredness after a hard day at work. I came up with the bright idea to have a bit of fun by seeing if I could break the Standing and Routine Orders for the barracks without being caught. Standing and Routine Orders are day to day things that need to get done, from something as simple as making your bed every day to checking certain pieces of equipment. Orders vary depending upon your trade specialty, or your Commanding Officer's preference in some barracks.

Lorraine and two of my other friends had watched me break a couple and found the whole thing very amusing. One example was, there used to be Fire buckets placed along the verandah, alternately one kept full of sand, one with water and so on. The sign read 'Do Not Touch The Buckets'. One day, as I walked past the buckets, I jumped from water bucket to sand bucket, all along the verandah until I had jumped in them all.

My friends wanted to get in on the action and help. I wasn't so sure, but Lorraine, Ronnie, and Kaye persuaded me, and the three Amigos became my partners in crime. As I thought, the first time ended up not being such a good idea. We made a quick plan and off we went and were promptly caught in the process of running a bra up the flag pole.

A Standing Order was implemented: 'Where a soldier is caught breaking a routine order, they shall be confined to Barracks for a period determined by their superior officer.'

Our confinement to barracks was accompanied by a punishment: wash and polish the floor in the main building – not with the industrial cleaner – using a cloth and bucket, on our hands and knees.

I did get caught again and the inevitable punishment meted-out: one time having to cut the lawn with a pair of scissors, another to paint the fence with a toothbrush. You would think that common sense would prevail and I would give up? Not me. I kept going until I had broken all the Routine Orders.

After lights out and bed check, Lorraine, Ronnie, Kaye, our other friend, Leslie, and myself, would sneak down the back steps and go and sit by the river, often drinking UDL cans we had stashed there prior. We never got caught partaking in that little escapade.

The Three Amigos and I would regularly get a pass from barracks at the weekend, catch the bus and visit Surfers Paradise. We spent our time during the days swimming and sunbathing. At night we listened to bands. I met Keith, a regular soldier from 6RAR, at one of the clubs and started our romance. I fell for the hint of mischief in his sparkling blue eyes and his wide cheesy grin. He was based at 6RAR Enoggera, Brisbane, which made it easy to catch up during the week for dinner, movies and walks. We often spent our weekends at Surfers Paradise, and once in a while the girls would join us.

On occasion, the girls and I would go to Stradbroke Island on the ferry. One side of the island housed a small community and a well-patronised, lively pub. We used to take our tents, with plenty of tinned food, to the other side of the island where we could camp and laze on the beach. One Sunday, we decided to walk to the pub for the Sunday session, which was packed. We were stood in our own little group as usual when two men to the side of me started having an argument. One of them threw a punch. The other man ducked but the punch hit a target, my face. The punch knocked me out. We never went to that side of the island again.

In the front of the building at Chelmer was a large lounge

where we were allowed to invite and host guests. One night, three of us invited three soldiers we knew from 6RAR, including Keith, over to our barracks for drinks. The evening was going well and we were enjoying the dancing and chatting when the canteen closed its doors. We were taken aback as it was early and we weren't ready to call it a night.

'Don't worry … I know where there are half a dozen beers,' I said. I beckoned to my two girlfriends to come with me and help. I knew there were six bottles of beer in the kitchen walk-in fridge. That they belonged to the Sergeants' Mess didn't deter me. We managed to open the crate and took the beer out; carefully opened the tops and emptied the beer out into jugs. We refilled the bottles with water, put the tops back on and put the bottles back in the crate and into the fridge. Our night was a great success.

All was well until a couple of days later. I came back to barracks from work to be met at the steps by Warrant Officer Townsend. She stood with her arms straight at her side, hands clenched, her face contorted in rage. I imagined any minute smoke would start emanating from her nose and ears. I had to keep a very straight face and stifle the smile that was forcing its way to my lips.

'Fuller told me you took the beer from the Sergeants' Mess fridge,' she snarled at me from clenched teeth. 'You are in lockdown, Crooks. March.'

I followed her, marching, to a small dingy room.

'In there!' she pointed.

I stepped inside. She shut and locked the door behind me.

'You will be escorted from here to work and back here after work for three days,' she said.

I sat on the bed, listening to her receding footsteps.

I hated that tiny room. But the experience did little to change my behaviour.

Lorraine confessed to me, once I was released from the hole – she had told Warrant Officer Townsend of our escapade after the bottles of water had been found. When Townsend was trying to find out who had done the deed, Lorraine told Townsend I swapped the beer for water by myself. It explained why I was the only one punished.

Ronnie and I were picked in the swimming squad to participate in the Inter-Service Sports. We always did well, but on the day of our competition, we weren't picked in the competing team. It was our punishment for our antics in the training session. In unison, we both flipped onto our backs and lifted our arms and legs skywards, and slowly sank. We were playing Dead Ants.

I received my first promotion while in Queensland, being notified of my promotion to Corporal one Friday. The following Monday, I was demoted back to Private. I was offered officer training several times during my enlistment but declined each time.

The Anzac Day march was always special to me. One year following the march, my platoon was taken to a lovely park for a barbeque lunch. I was walking across the lawn when my foot caught in a divot and my ankle twisted. The pain was excruciating and I sat holding and gently rubbing it. One of my friends told me to leave my shoe on for support and get it checked out back at the barracks. I managed to last the day, despite the constant ache.

Back at the barracks, I took off my shoe to reveal my swollen and now black ankle. My friends kept telling me to hurry up as they were eager to get going, a night on the town beckoning. I got out of my uniform, put on casual clothes and joined them. But the pain didn't go away so I took myself home early. I didn't sleep well as even the sheet touching my foot was painful.

The next day I dressed for work and sought a lift with one of the other girls who had borrowed her boyfriend's Monaro. Every time we hit a bump, I almost went through the roof. Once at my unit, I waited another hour for somebody to take me to the RAP (Regimental Aide Post). The medic looked at my ankle.

'You need an x-ray," the medic diagnosed. 'Go to Wacol Army Hospital. Can you get yourself there?'

'Does it look like I can?' I asked. The hospital was miles away.

The medic arranged for someone to take me, although the wait was quite a while. When I eventually got to the hospital, I was in serious pain. After the x-ray was taken, I sat outside on a wooden bench to wait for the results. More time passed and someone eventually stuck their head out the window.

'Private Crooks, your ankle is broken. Just walk up the hill over there, take the first turn to the left, then turn right. You'll see the Q store where you can get crutches. Once you have the crutches, come back here and the doctor will see you,' he said. I looked at him in disbelief. 'When you get back, we'll set it. It will need plaster,' he said and shut the window.

After many tears and a lot of pain, I made it to the Q Store, got the crutches, and started to make my way back. I had great trouble managing the crutches and almost fell and broke my other ankle. I made it back to where I needed to be.

The doctor did set my ankle, putting on a plaster cast to my knee. He explained the small rest heel was exactly that, a small heel for me to rest my leg, not to walk on.

I was driven back to Chelmer where I found everyone getting ready to go to a party. No show without Punch, I got ready and went with them. Of course, I couldn't resist and joined everyone on the dance floor for *Let's Twist Again*. Next morning my leg was so swollen I had to go back to the hospital. The plaster was replaced with a new one, minus the little heel.

I wasn't given a medical certificate for time off work, the assumption being I had a desk job. No one asked and I didn't think to volunteer the information that I was a driver. I went to work, but immediately there was a real problem – depressing the clutch in a 1960's Land Rover with a plastered left leg? … it wasn't going to happen.

I worked out to place one crutch onto the clutch, to push and hold it down, engage first gear then accelerate. The one thing left to be done was to get the revs right and change gears. This proved successful, nevertheless with a lot of grinding. This worked well when the car was moving; stopping was another matter. I held my right foot hard on the brake and let the Land Rover stall, then repeated the crutch manoeuvre to get going again. I became a master doing this for the six weeks my leg was in plaster.

In 1964 Australia introduced a scheme of selective conscription and committed troops to be sent to Vietnam in 1965. In May 1966, Keith told me that 6RAR was being deployed for their first six-month tour of Vietnam but didn't know the exact date they were going. We met as often as we could. Without warning, and under strict secrecy, partly due to the increasing demonstrations in Australia against the Vietnam war, 6RAR battalion embarked on the HMAS

Sydney, under the dark of night, and the ship stole away.

There was a lot of graffiti on buildings opposing the Vietnam war, and one caught my eye. Someone had written on the wall "DISARM TODAY". Someone else came along and wrote underneath it, "DAT ARM TOMORROW".

November 1966 Keith returned from Vietnam to 6RAR barracks in Enoggera. I met him as soon as I could. We met several times but the Vietnam War had changed him, as it did many young Australian men. There was both an urgency and a wariness about him. We tried to make our relationship work but it proved too difficult and we drifted apart.

By the end of November, I was posted to 101 Randwick in Sydney, still as a driver. I returned to barracks at Georges Heights and again bussed to and from work. 101 Randwick supplied vehicles and drivers to officers and other personnel with a few other jobs, including army mail runs.

There were three mail runs. I was assigned the Blue Mail run, and given a VW Kombi van with a bench seat and floor gear shift. The first job of the day was to pick up the mail from Victoria Barracks in Paddington before following the regular route of the Blue Mail run to drop off mail and pick-up mail for posting and drop off back at Paddington.

My driver's uniform was a pair of issue slacks, an army shirt and tie and a battle jacket. The legs of the slacks were wide – very wide on my small frame. I was highly organised and my routine ran like clockwork. First, I put the mail in order of drop off location, neatly stacked on the front seat next to me. Second, I pulled up at one of my stops, jumped out of the van, dropped off the mail, picked up outgoing mail. Third, I jumped back into the Kombi, put the mail in the back, hit the clutch and gear stick in one movement and take off, all before the door of the van was closed.

One day, at one of my stops, a Lieutenant was waiting next to the mail.

'I'm coming with you, Private. I need to go to Victoria Barracks,' he stated.

'Sorry, sir. I'm not allowed to take passengers. You will need to contact Randwick for a driver,' I said.

'This is a command, Private! You will take me to the barracks,' he said.

'Sir, this isn't the last stop of the mail run. I still have a long way to go. I'm not going straight there,' I informed him, thinking he would seek an alternative.

'Complete your run; I'll come with you,' he said.

I had no choice – I had to take him. To make matters worse, he insisted on sitting in the front of the van, so I had to move the mail.

At my next stop, I jumped out, retrieved the mail from the back of the van, my routine now totally out of whack. I took the mail into the mailroom, picked up the outgoing mail and, back at the van, did my usual jump back into the Kombi.

My left hand flayed about looking for the gear stick. Taken aback that it wasn't where I thought it was, I started looking, panic rising in my throat. *Where's my gear stick?*

I noticed the officer looking at me. Then he spoke, 'It's up the leg of your trousers.'

With great embarrassment, I lifted my leg and found my gearstick. I took my time for the remainder of the run.

When the mail run finished, the routine involved sitting in a waiting room to wait for an order to come in. If there were a few of us, we played cards or read until needed. The pool of cars were sedans, staff cars and Holden Utilities. We received an order one day to transport two Generals to the city. I was the only driver in the room, with only one vehicle left in the pool, which posed a problem. The Routine Order involving a high-ranking officer required a staff car with five stars, just above the front bumper, uncovered, and one flag on each side of the bonnet. The only vehicle left in the pool was a Holden utility. No stars. No flags.

The officers declined to wait for a staff car. I was ordered to take them both in the utility. The gear stick in the utility is a column shift, the seating a bench seat. The other Routine Order for transporting high ranking officers involves alerting the guards at the barrack gates of the rank of the officer by giving a certain number of toots as you approach the gate. Generals were three toots, and the guards would present arms, the Generals would salute, and the driver gently drove on while the Generals held their salute until we passed the guard.

As we approached the gates of Victoria Barracks, I tooted three times. The guard appeared and presented arms, which takes a few seconds. I waited with my hand on the gear stick. The General sitting next to me raised his arm to salute, but hooked his arm through my arm, which jarred the gearstick and the gears changed to neutral.

'Move on, driver,' the General said.

My arm was still looped by his, and I could barely move. I valiantly lifted the gear stick then gritted my teeth, ready to pull it down into gear, all the while with the General repeating 'Move on, driver'. The guard saw what was happening and worked hard to keep the smile off his face. With the General's saluting arm wrapped around my arm, I pulled down on the gear stick, pulling the General's arm down, along with his head, which whacked into the steering wheel. He ended up with a bleeding nose. I kept my eyes fixed straight ahead and no one spoke.

My car on the Blue Mail run was changed from the Kombi van to a Holden Utility. One of the guys at one of the stops used to collect coupons from boxes of soap powder. Rather than wait 'till one box was empty he would open several at a time, leaving him with many open packets of soap powder. One of my first stops with the utility was where the soap box guy worked.

'Crooks, would you like a couple of boxes of soap powder?' he asked.

'Thanks, I will. What, maybe three boxes?' I replied.

He handed them to me and I carefully put them in the space at the back of the seat, just behind my head.

I drove along Military Road and saw a car on the opposite side of the road, waiting to turn right. I got level with it and for some reason, the driver turned the car and hit the driver's door of my car. The driver of the other car must have put their foot down on the accelerator as the subsequent impact with my car caused it to roll over. It settled on its side. My lap seat belt worked well, but I was now up in the air, hanging towards the passenger side of the vehicle. The soap powder escaped the open boxes and was all over the car cabin. I started violently sneezing. Every time I sneezed, I hit my head on the steering wheel.

Some men stopped to help and got me out of the car. They thought I was badly hurt as there was a lot of blood. They soon saw the blood was coming from my battered nose.

'I'm fine. I'm fine. Thank you,' I kept saying.

'Does your thumb always stick out at that angle?' someone asked, pointing to my hand.

I looked down and saw my thumb was at right angles to my hand. I passed out.

After I had been in NSW for about three months, Lorraine was transferred to 101 Randwick. I had my best mate back again. Sometimes we were allowed to take our vehicles home to Georges Heights for the night. If there were three of us, each with our vehicle, we would get onto the Sydney Harbour Bridge, and each take one of the three lanes. We then slowed down, holding up the homeward-bound traffic. It was just the devil in us.

I remained working at Randwick and was due for discharge in June 1967. I was about to re-enlist for another three years but, when I applied for leave to attend my sister's wedding, my application was denied.

I left the regular army.

In early 1966, while I was still in the Army, Mum and Dad were in financial trouble and lost the house in Wonthella. They moved to a four-room statehouse in Beachlands. It had two bedrooms, a tiny lounge and kitchen, which was a far cry from our house in Wonthella, so Mum was back to a tiny house. Never once did she complain – she just got on with it and made it a home. Dad filled in part of the front verandah to make a bedroom for when I came home from the army.

On Leave December 1964

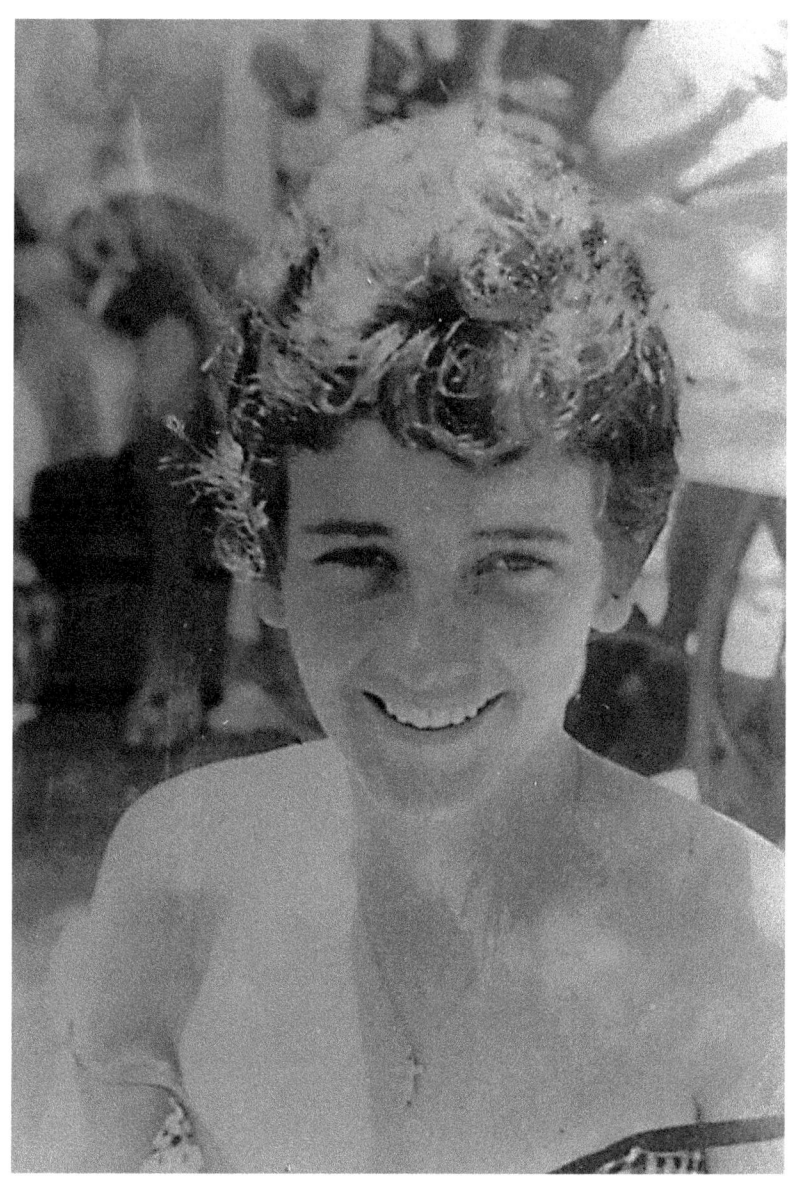

Me 1964

ID Photo 1965

Me at Surfers Paradise 1965

Keith & I Surfers 1965

Surfers 1965

Keith and I 1965

Me, 1966 Queensland

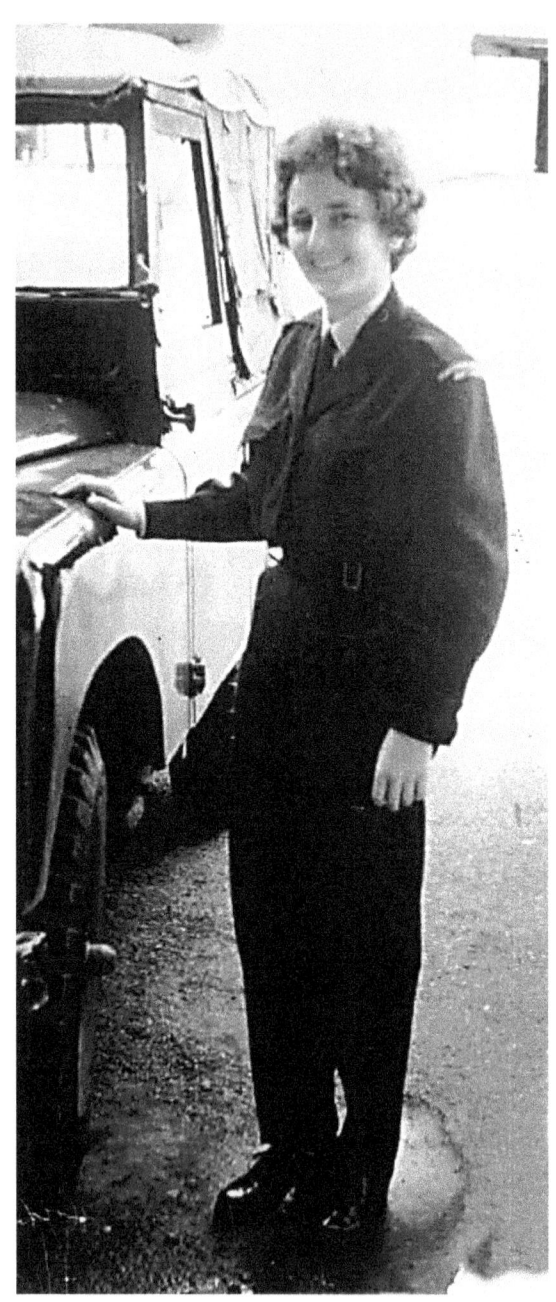
Me, 1966 Queensland

Chapter 7: Army Reserves and 'Civvy' Street

I went home to Geraldton and celebrated with Annette and Tom on their wedding day. They settled into their family life, soon welcoming two children, Mathew in 1968 and Tracey in 1970. Now I had left the Army, my family encouraged me to settle in Geraldton but I wasn't done with travel and opted to move to Perth. My first job in Perth was as a bread carter. It didn't take me long to work out that I needed something a little more meaningful. I chose to study accounting via correspondence through Stotts College.

After a few clerical positions, I started work as a casual, through a company that provided clerical staff for temporary positions, such as leave relief or during busy periods. I was given plenty of work and always had three or four jobs lined up. I was sent to one business to sort out a large backlog of invoices and get the cash flow back on track. I worked there for three weeks and then moved on to the next job.

Within the first week, the owner of the previous business contacted me privately and offered me a full-time position as the accountant in his firm. I accepted the offer and stayed with him for twenty-five years, most of that time as the Group Accountant. While one of my goals was to travel, I hadn't envisaged travelling for business, but that's what happened. The business grew, and a fair bit of my time was spent on business trips, both national and international. I worked hard and certainly enjoyed the travel component.

Although I was settled and involved in my work, I missed the Army. The Army Reserves was a good option for me, and I joined in late 1969. The Reserves was part-time: every Tuesday night, most weekends and twice per year – two full weeks away, playing war games. I loved it, even though sometimes it was hard keeping up with my full-time job and travel commitments. I particularly enjoyed learning and using a self-loading rifle, SLR, although doing parades with the rifle was hard work as they are heavy.

After my years in the regular army and settled in a responsible position as an accountant in civvy street, I was confident and comfortable. My mischievous sense of fun hadn't changed much in the years since my Regular Army days – it was now enhanced with my strong sense of self-reliance. Needless to say, I always seemed to be in trouble with my superiors. There was one added complication. Many of the officers were part-time soldiers themselves, with no previous Army experience.

On one two-week camp, my platoon was deployed to a forest camp in the south of Western Australia. One day, fifteen troops were sent on a reconnaissance mission. I hadn't been under the charge of the Lieutenant, and others hadn't seen him in our battalion before. We were told the plan was to be back at base by 1400 hours. We were given rations for lunch and marched off, as planned, at 0800 hours.

I started getting worried when I saw the Lieutenant put his compass on the barrel of his rifle, check it, then point, 'This way.'

My sense of direction is very good, and after six hours of traipsing around in the bush, I knew we were lost. So, I spoke up.

'Sir! Do you think we should be heading back this way?' I asked, pointing my finger in the opposite direction to where he was about to go.

'It's this way, Crooks,' he said.

'I don't think so, sir,' I offered. 'I'm sure camp's this way, sir.'

'Don't argue, Crooks. I know what I am doing. This is the way back to camp. Get on with it, this way, Crooks,' he said and walked off.

I'd had enough. I turned around and walked off in the opposite direction. I heard him yelling after me.

'Crooks! Get back here or you will be charged with disobeying a direct order.'

I ignored him.

I walked on a short way and turned to see if he had changed his mind, as I wasn't about to change mine. I was surprised to see eight soldiers following me.

We made it back to camp long before dark.

The Commanding Officer saw us struggle into camp and strode over to our group.

'Where is the Lieutenant and the others?' he asked

'I don't know, sir,' I replied. 'I left, as the Lieutenant didn't seem to know where he was going. These soldiers chose to follow me, sir.'

The Lieutenant and the other soldiers didn't return. A search party was sent out the next morning, with a helicopter assisting. They were all found safe and well.

I saw the Lieutenant go to the Commanding Officer's Mess. I grew impatient so I marched to the Mess and knocked on the door.

'Come. What is it, Crooks?' the Commanding Officer asked when he saw me.

'Sir. The Lieutenant said I would be charged for disobeying his order. I am wondering when the charge is likely to be issued?'

The Commanding Officer coughed and looked at the Lieutenant. 'Get on with it, Crooks. No charge … this time.'

Another two-week camp, this one in Northam, saw me again at odds with an officer.

Each Sunday morning is a church parade; they are voluntary and I tended to opt-out. One Sunday, ten other soldiers joined me.

We were taking the opportunity to have a rest from marching and exercises, lying on our beds, some reading, others snoozing. The Duty Adjutant marched into the barracks.

'Get your packs on, pick up your weapons, meet me on the parade ground. Now! C'mon, get moving!' he barked.

We jumped to it.

The parade ground is at the foot of a hill. Once there, he ordered us to run around the perimeter of the parade ground in full kit. He made the mistake of berating us for not going to the church parade and told us this was our punishment.

I declined to participate, turned and marched back up the hill. I heard him yelling and calling me.

I saw the Colonel, our Commanding Officer, coming toward me. As he drew close, I saluted.

'Crooks,' he called. I stopped marching.

'Crooks, can't you hear the Adjutant calling you?' he asked.

'Yes, sir! He told us this was our punishment for not attending the church parade. He can't do that, sir!' I explained.

The Colonel nodded and sent me on my way. Within minutes all the others were on their way back to our huts. I heard the Adjutant copped an earful and a warning.

I was tasked one day with preparing the mess area for one of the meals. I couldn't find any cups or saucers and decided the best course of action was to borrow some from the officers' mess. I popped several cups and saucers into my shirt and headed back to the soldiers' mess. I clunked as I passed the Colonel.

'Private Crooks,' he called, 'anything you want to tell me about?'

'No, sir,' I replied.

'What do you have in your shirt?'

'Cups and saucers, sir.'

'Why?'

'We don't have any.'

'Why didn't you go through the correct channels, Crooks?'

'Too much paperwork, sir.'

He shook his head. 'Get on with it, Crooks.'

During my time in the Reserves, I was promoted to Temporary Corporal for three months, then another promotion to Temporary Sergeant. One week later, I was demoted back to Private for being smart and back chatting someone higher ranked. I remained a Private for my time in the Reserves.

Consequently, no one was more surprised than I when I was nominated for, and won, Soldier of the Year. I was to receive my commemorative award at the end of year parade. I practised my march onto the dais, stood to attention in front of the Colonel, took the award, saluted, then about-turned and marched back into line.

On the day of the parade, I made sure my uniform was spotless, the creases ironed extra sharp. I polished my boots so well no self-respecting speck of dust would dare settle on them. I knew my parents were at the parade and I held my shoulders back and head high. The award was announced.

I marched forward, came to attention and touched the rifle barrel – the normal salute in the Army when you carry a weapon – in front of the Colonel.

'Well done, Private Crooks,' he said, handing me the award.

I took the award. Then stared open-mouthed at the Colonel. I had given no thought to how I was going to salute with the award in my left hand and weapon in my right. *If I salute, I'll either drop the award or knock myself out.* I looked at the award, looked back at the Colonel.

'How do you think I should do this, sir?' I whispered.

'Just about-turn and go, Crooks,' he said.

Following the parade, my parents and I were enjoying drinks and finger food. I was with a group of friends, standing behind my father when the Colonel joined my parents.

I overheard the Colonel say, 'She's a born leader and a very good soldier, you know. But …'

Interjecting, my father said, 'Yes, there's always a *BUT* with Denise.'

They both laughed. I smiled too, comfortable, knowing my dad was proud of me.

I resigned from the Army Reserves in 1984, aged 39. I thought eighteen years' service, notwithstanding a two-year break between the Regular Army and Reserves, was about enough. Besides, I felt I was getting on a bit; the energy for the exercise was waning.

Post my time in the Reserves, I thought I needed a break

from accounting and tried my hand at running a liquor store. I took time doing my due diligence; checked the accounts and associated paperwork; visited the relevant government departments and spent some time with the owner. As the final transaction was going through, the business owner and four of his friends were tragically killed in an aeroplane crash near Geraldton. They had been on a fishing trip to Shark Bay.

Having a liquor store is hard work, and I was always pushed for time. Every Sunday I would drive down to the post box to post the cheque for the beer delivery, which had to be received by the brewery by Tuesday to enable my next beer delivery. One Sunday, I was really, really busy and drove to the post box with about a minute to spare before the box was emptied. I pulled the car up, jumped out and posted the cheque, jumped back into the car and thought: "Damn! Someone has stolen my steering wheel." I sat there for a moment then realised I was sitting in the back seat.

All was going well for me until eight months into running the store. I received an $85,000 bill from the Liquor Licensing Commission for incorrect Liquor License returns from the previous two years. At the same time, and unbeknown to me, the police were in the middle of a criminal inquiry, which had been in progress for a while. The previous owner, apparently, had other liquor stores and used to purchase liquor for my store under the license of one of his other stores. Which is illegal.

I immediately went and worked it out with my bank. I didn't go into bankruptcy but lost my house, which I sold to pay off the debt. I got through the experience and gradually got back on my feet. I was extremely fortunate that my old boss wanted me back and resumed my position of group accountant.

In 1968 Mum and Dad bought a small fishing shack at Snag Island, now known as Leeman. Dad took his boat and made Snag his base. They were amongst the first fishermen to live there. My parents loved it at Snag, and often, particularly on weekends and Easter, I would go to Snag and go crayfishing with Dad. When we finished pulling cray pots, we would just drift and line fish for dhufish and snapper.

When they first moved to Snag, Mum was back to having no running water or electricity. The rainwater tank was filled from rain running from the roof of the shack and electricity was from our own generator. Not long after they settled in, Dad fixed running water to the kitchen sink from the rainwater tank and water to the shower from a bore. Snag, to me at the time, was the best place on earth and an easy place to visit, only a couple of hundred kilometres from Perth. We had so much fun there fishing most of the day and in the evening playing scrabble.

When I wasn't crayfishing with Dad, I would still go with him to the boat with the dinghy. On one occasion, when we got to Compass Rose, he noticed the outboard of the dinghy was very low on petrol. As he climbed onto the boat, I tossed him the dinghy rope and he threw it over the cray pot winch. He lowered the petrol can and, while I filled the dinghy tank, he started to get Compass Rose ready for the day's fishing.

'Denise, you nearly done?' he asked.

I looked up at him and didn't get the chance to answer as my head kept moving and before I knew it, the petrol can and I were in the water, looking up at the suspended dinghy.

Dad had accidentally started the winch and lifted the

dinghy out of the water.

'Sorry, love,' Dad yelled, 'I'll drop the dinghy back, watch yourself.'

The dinghy resumed its place in the water next to Compass Rose.

'Dad, help me get back in,' I shouted

He looked down at me treading water, then across at the boat.

'You'll manage to get back in. You'll be okay,' he said, disappearing for a moment before returning with a boat hook to retrieve the petrol can.

In 1972 Dad sold his crayfishing outfit, including the shack at Snag and both Mum and Dad moved to Perth. They bought a house not far from where I lived.

Dad still wanted to work, so got a job as a car salesman – he always was a charmer – and he adapted very well and did a good job, until his retirement in 1975. My parents bought a caravan and a new dinghy and spent their early retirement years sharing time between winter in Exmouth and summer in Perth.

In 1991, Dad suffered his first heart attack, followed by bypass surgery. This, unfortunately, ended his annual travel to Exmouth. Dad continued to suffer problems with his heart, and ultimately a pacemaker was needed.

In their later years, while Mum and Dad were living with me, we were going out shopping. I went to their bedroom to see if they were ready and stood at the door – they didn't know I was there. Mum was sitting on the bed and Dad was kneeling down to help her put her stockings on when he said to her, "Oh, you still have such beautiful legs.

Mum and Dad made sure they made frequent visits to Geraldton to see Annette, Tom and the grandchildren, and subsequently their great-grandchildren, as Mathew and Tracey married and welcomed their own offspring.

Mum and Dad agreed to move in with me when they were both aged 85. Dad's and Mum's health gradually faded and they both died in 2003, within ten days of each other, both two months short of their 86th birthday.

Annette and Tom on their wedding day

Annette and I on her wedding day

Mum and I 1994

Mum, Dad, Annette and I 1994

Lorraine and I today

Epilogue

I smiled to myself. Our early years in Australia were certainly challenging but fun. We shared fantastic memories and good times.

My good times and fun continued in the army with great friends. I looked at the letter I was spinning in my hand; stopped spinning it; turned it over, and opened it. My smile widened. Yes. I had the correct address, and Lorraine was looking forward to catching up.

I called her the next day and we laughed and chatted, swapped email addresses and promised to keep in touch.

I shouldn't be surprised a letter would have far-reaching consequences as there were a few in my early years that taught me otherwise.

Lorraine visited me in Geraldton and didn't return to Adelaide. We made our home in the northern suburbs of Perth, leaving Geraldton in June 2018.

Lorraine is keen for me to share stories about my successful career as an accountant.

But that is a story for another time …

Acknowledgements

In a life well-lived, there are always many people to thank for their support, their willingness to share the good times, as well as the not so good, and to help when called upon. Thank you to friends, family, workmates, puppy dogs for being who you are, for being there.

Thank you to Helen Iles for your publishing advice and getting my memoir to print.

Special thanks to Sandra Smiles. Without your invaluable assistance, my story would never have seen the light of day.

About the Author

Denise Crooks was born in England in 1945 and emigrated with her family to Australia in 1950, settling in Geraldton, Western Australia

Denise is very family orientated. She grew up loving the ocean and fishing and living the idyllic life of a crayfisherman's daughter, often getting herself into various hilarious situations. She went on to become an accountant and successful businesswoman. Denise is an avid animal lover – dogs especially are one of her passions. She also loves woodwork and is quite adept at making wooden toys and furniture for family and friends.

Denise has spent many years in the military, both full time and part-time.

She decided to write this book to show the other side of this successful businesswoman with a wicked sense of humour.

www.ingramcontent.com/pod-product-compliance
Lightning Source LLC
LaVergne TN
LVHW051225070526
838200LV00057B/4607